ANCE

VENERATION

Connecting with Your Ancestors, Spirit Guides and Guardian Angels and Honoring Them

MYSTIC MAE

About the Author

Mystic Mae is a senior coach at Mindset Mastership, a life coaching business based in London, England.

Mindset Mastership teaches clients how human behavior really works.

Through our teaching, we have helped client's worldwide gain a better advantage, to develop themselves and achieve more from life.

We'e in the changing lives business.

Want Free New Book Launches?

Email us at:

mindsetmastership@gmail.com

& Follow us on Instagram!

@MindsetMastership

MASTERSHIP BOOKS

UK | USA | Canada | Ireland | Australia

India | New Zealand | South Africa | China

Mastership Books is part of the United Arts Publishing House group of companies based in London, England, UK.

First published by Mastership Books (London, UK), 2022

I S B N: 978-1-915002-23-5

Text Copyright © United Arts Publishing

Cover design by Rich © United Arts Publishing (UK)

Text and internal design by Rich © United Arts Publishing (UK)

Image credits reserved.

Colour separation by Spitting Image Design Studio

Printed and bound in Great Britain

National Publications Association of Britain

London, England, United Kingdom.

Paper design UAP

ISBN: 978-1-915002-23-5 (paperback)

A723.5

Title: ANIMAL SPIRIT GUIDES

Design, Bound & Printed:

London, England,

Great Britain.

Mindfulness, Meditation Spirituality Books

"Wherever you go, go with all your heart."

— **Confucius**

GET A FREE AUDIOBOOK

EMAIL SUBJECT LINE:

"ANCESTRAL VENERATION"

TO

MINDSETMASTERSHIP@GMAIL.COM

ANCESTRAL VENERATION

*Connecting with Your Ancestors, Spirit Guides
and Guardian Angels and Honoring Them*

CONTENTS

Chapter 1

Spiritual Practices For Beginners: How To Begin Connecting With Your Ancestors

A s a child, my father once told me, "You must understand your origins to understand your destination." Because I was still in a young person in high school, I ignored what he said. However, that phrase carries a lot of weight now. And that was echoed following my grandma's death.

You've arrived here because you're curious about how to initiate a spiritual connection with your ancestors. You're ready to take your ancestral devotion work to the next level and extend your spiritual practice. However, when starting the procedure "properly," you may be unsure. Working with your ancestors does not have a one-size-fits-all strategy. But by following the compass of your intuitive direction, the process is entirely up to you.

However, advice can be made to help overcome self-doubt along the way. Connecting with your ancestors is a self-healing process. The methods from this book can aid in resolving generational trauma and facilitating access to generational gifts.

Let go of any guilt or shame that may accompany your foray into spirituality by reading the following advice, which is meant to inspire you to start connecting with your ancestors.

Recognizing the Past

Whether you are a first-generation Latina or a fourth-generation European, regardless of where you fit on the spectrum, there is a communal barrier to overcome when connecting with ancestors. This is referred to as assimilation. Our relatives who moved to the United States were forced to survive by conforming to a new type of "American culture." This entails speaking less of our native language, engaging in more American cultural customs, and so forth, and leaving fragmented access to our past.

It can be perplexing, isolated, and lonely when attempting to trace your ancestors, let alone commemorate their history. Occasionally, there is little to go on when tracing your ancestors for various reasons. However, avoid being too fixated on that. Instead, recognizing the past entails respecting the place you live and the land walked by your forefathers and mothers. You can expand your family tree, take a DNA test, and request oral histories.

All you have to do is begin acknowledging your family's history. The positive, the negative, and the ugly. As unbearable as it may sound. We must embrace it all, as truth, but with positivity.

Don't Be Afraid to Talk to the Dead.

To begin reconnecting with your ancestors, we ..... decolonizing our worldview. As Euro-centric people, we have been brainwashed with fear. Fear of communicating with the dead or working with the Dead has numerous stigmas.

"PERHAPS YOU DID NOT WANT TO SPEAK TO THE DEAD TO AVOID BEING PERCEIVED AS "CRAZY," TODAYS CULTURE ALREADY STIGMATIZES MENTAL HEALTH. PERHAPS YOU GREW UP IN AN OVERLY RELIGIOUS HOUSEHOLD, WHERE WORKING WITH SPIRITS WAS VIEWED AS "DEMONIC". WELL, TIME TO ELIMINATE FEAR."

How? Work through the internalized narratives derived from this extreme religious and materialistic culture within you. Communicating with our past ancestors often manifests feminine energy—a state of intuition, receptivity, and stillness. We were trained to despise and dismiss these behaviors to sustain euro-american-capitalist control and thus focus on work and materialism.

You will not be harmed by the our past elders. Establish clear boundaries with Spirit and your higher power to only connect with ancestors looking out for your best interests. Choose a guardian spirit to defend you from low-energy spirits by inviting them into your altar area or invoking him in prayers. This could include Archangels or animal spirit guardians. It is all up to you.

We attract low vibratory experiences and vibrations when we dwell in fear. In the realm of the spirits, this is especially true. The darkness is real, but so is the greater brightness. So declare your limits with the realm of Spirit out loud.

Reclaim Your Traditions

Connecting with your ancestors is an intensely personal and one-of-a-kind experience. Consequently, your ancestral practice will be distinct from those of others. Consider prioritizing your culture's and immediate family's traditions when you build or deepen your ancestral practice. While it may feel natural to incorporate frameworks from other practitioners' practices into your own, trust that your intuitive guidance and the traditions of your immediate ancestral lineages will strengthen your practice.

Ask living family members whether they have any recipes or rituals to pass on to you. It is beneficial to solicit oral histories from current seniors about what they recall their elders doing in their personal spiritual and ancestral worship activities. Allow yourself to adapt or eliminate those that do not resonate with you.

Reclaiming is a remembrance act. At times, tracing one's ancestors might be difficult, including assimilation, trauma, and more. Nevertheless, the desire to regain your traditions is an admirable goal and a simple approach to invoke the spirits of your forefathers and mothers as an expression of appreciation.

Equally, research the heritage your ancestors came from and the cultural traditions that stem from your lineage. Simultaneously, observe how your current living seniors (future ancestors) live and any customs you wish to learn from them to pass on to future generations. This establishes a connection between you and the deceased and vice versa.

Work with Living Elders

I always question my students, "Why to wait till your family members are deceased before beginning to work with or venerate them?" Collaborating with living seniors, who are essentially our forefathers and mothers, is a proactive method to maintain a connection to our ancestors. Additionally, this aim aids in strengthening relationships transferred into the afterlife.

You may be wondering if an ancestor with whom you were not in contact or who you never met will manifest in Spirit. Usually, they will. Unless they never crossed over or were unconvinced of the validity of this effort. They are unlikely to throw you a welcome party if you invite them into your spiritual activity.

You do not have to be related directly to an ancestor for them to desire to cooperate with you. However, having a previous repertoire helps tremendously bring them in faster.

Collaborating with living ancestors enables us to initiate intergenerational healing cooperatively. Inquire of your living elders about their stories. Inquire about their traumas and happy recollections. This is how you can begin assisting them in alleviating the burden of heavy karma before their transfer to the afterlife.

Calling in Your Ancestral Lineage in Spirit

To begin summoning your ancestors, consider doing so as part of the process of erecting an altar, praying, or performing ceremonial activities. Then, by leaving them offerings, you can invite them into your home.

Offerings might range from their favorite cuisine to a commitment made in their honor that you will keep. Constructing an altar is an effective way to connect with them. Construct your altar by the requirements of your forefathers and mothers. What did they take pleasure in while they were alive? Which flowers were they particularly fond of? Were they coffee or tequila drinkers? Leave those out as offerings to them to demonstrate your intention to develop a spiritual relationship with them.

Along with prayer, the simplest and quickest approach to sense your ancestors' presence is likely to be through meditation. Take 10-30 minutes to sit in meditation and especially bring in the ancestor to whom you feel the strongest connection and invite them to speak with you!

Additionally, lighting a candle is a means to invoke their Spirit. Designating specific candles for your ancestors on a year-round basis maybe something they like. Make it a stride further and get a candle in their beloved tone to communicate your availability to draw in with them. Celebrating their birthdays by preparing a special dinner for them or lighting a candle on major anniversaries is also an excellent way to co-create a dynamic with them.

Finally, solicit guidance and direction from your intuition. Additionally, you can inquire about how family members perform this work personally. It could be as easy as paying more frequent visits to loved ones' graves. Connecting with your ancestors will take on a variety of forms. When dealing with them, the only thing that matters is the intention. Where do your motives originate? Are they sincere and compassionate? Are they purely self-serving? In any case, take pleasure in the procedure!

Chapter 2

The Different Kinds Of Spirit Guides And How To Communicate With Them

Nobody can deny the existence of spirit guides who are always talking with them. Here, you'll learn how to identify your guides, open yourself up to their wisdom, and communicate with them at any time.

What types of spirit guides are there?

Certain spirit guides had accompanied you throughout your life, even before you were born. Others joined your team as you required them at various points in your life, and you can continue to utilize your free will to request additional spirit guides.

Your spiritual guidance squad, the group of spirit guides that have been allocated to you, may contain any or all of the following:

Archangels

Archangels are the leaders of the angelic realm and possess a tremendously powerful energy signature. If you are an empath or are sensitive to energy, you may notice a shift in the energy in the room when you invoke an archangel. Each archangel has a specialty, such as Archangel Raphael's specialty of healing, and can work with an unlimited number of humans simultaneously.

Guardian angels

Guardian angels are entirely yours, and we have more than one! Guardian angels have dedicated their lives to assist you specifically. You can reach out to them at any time for instant assistance. They will always adore you unconditionally. Remember that angels are interfaith and work with individuals of all faiths and spiritual beliefs.

Spirit animals

Spirit animals maybe a pet who died and is now a member of your spiritual guiding squad. Your spirit animal could also be any animal that has taught you something, such as the value of beauty, how important it is to claim your gifts, or how important it is to meet your survival needs, like a peacock.

Spirit animals may manifest for the first time in a dream, in your backyard, or on the coffee mug.

Ascended masters

Ascended Masters such as Buddha or Mother Mary were once human beings who embarked on profound spiritual development and influence journeys. They now hold a unique position as spiritual leaders and guides/teachers to humans like you.

My guides have informed me that all ascended masters are partners and work in unison, regardless of the country or religion in which they lived.

Departed loved ones

Those who have passed on may choose to become one of your spirit guides and actively support you from the afterlife by supplying you with work possibilities or cultivating relationships.

One of your grandmothers could be a significant spirit guide for you, regardless of how well you knew her in life. Indeed, any human who has died may serve as a spirit guide for you. A spirit guide who was a dancer and performer in their own right may be on your team to help and inspire you as an artist.

Helper angels

Helper angels are "freelance angels" looking for people to assist them with certain tasks, such as making new acquaintances or locating a new office space.

What mode of communication do spirit guides use to connect with us?

Spirit guides frequently enter your life through signals, also known as synchronicities. The term "synchronicity" was coined by Carl Jung to describe "a striking coincidence." Consider the following scenario: you recognize the need to enhance your romantic relationship following a disagreement with your partner before bedtime. You notice a book about romantic relationship communication resting on a coworker's desk the next day. Numbers and sequences like 111 can also be used by your spirit guides to connect with you. For example, you might see a lucky number in the address of an interviewing business.

When you get into your car after a particularly trying day, you can hear a song that always lifts your spirits play on the radio.

Spirit guides may send you a dream that guides how to approach an issue, or they may appear to you in a dream. Another way your spirit guide communicates with you is by sending you help people and opportunities, which often necessitates that you take action in response to the person or opportunity your guide has sent or placed on your radar (e.g., inviting an interesting new person to lunch or purchasing a ticket to a transformational workshop).

Ten methods for initiating communication with your spirit guides.

The following are some practical techniques for establishing contact with your guiding squad and identifying their signs and synchronicities:

1. Make an effort to be more present in your daily life.

Recognize the signals your spirit guides are already sending. So often miss the signals our guides send us because our lives or minds are too busy.

Consider freeing up some space in your schedule or relieving yourself of some duties. When you're not hurrying around, you'll find that your guides send you more messages. To improve your capacity to clear your mind, find a meditation technique that you enjoy and can use often.

2. Be on the alert for signs from your guides every day.

The more attentive you are to your guides' signals, the more easily you recognize them. However, something else remarkable occurs— as you become more conscious of your guides and their beneficial messages, they will send you more.

Remind yourself daily that your guides communicate with you on your train journey to work or showering in the morning. Suppose you're attempting to make a significant decision or are experiencing significant changes or obstacles. In that case, you may anticipate an increase of guidance coming your way to assist you in navigating this scenario.

3. Begin a notebook for your spirit guides.

Purchase a dedicated diary and dedicate it entirely to improving communication between you and your advisors. Here you can write to your guardians and ask for their help in a specific way.

While your guides are well acquainted with you and your life, it can be extremely beneficial to utilize your free will to request assistance and advice. Additionally, you can use this journal to keep track of any significant signals they transmit.

Write a letter to your guides at the start of each week, expressing gratitude for a phrase or two about something in your life that you believe they've added recently. Then ask for assistance or advice on a specific topic in a few phrases. Finally, throughout the remainder of the week, keep an eye out for synchronicities from your guides regarding this matter.

4. Become acquainted with your guides and give them names.

You might choose a name for one of the guardian angels that you've always admired, such as Emily. Alternatively, you may be thinking of your guardian angel while you read the name Javier or Gigi in a novel, and that becomes their name. Giving your guide a name humanizes them and may motivate you to communicate with them more frequently. You may also understand one of your guides' personalities as you engage more closely with them over time.

Consider whether a name for one of your guides comes to you through intuition or synchronicity, or be creative and give them a name.

If a mentor constantly assists in advancing your profession, they may be serious and driven. On the other hand, another guide may be lighthearted and constantly provide hilarious advice, encouraging you to relax and enjoy the experience.

5. Make a gift to your guides.

When you're frustrated with a situation, unsure of the best course of action, or feel as though you lack control, turn the matter over to your guides. Even if it is only to give oneself a brief respite, this can allow for new ideas to come to you and provide your guides greater freedom to do their work and assist you.

Practice relinquishing an issue to your guides energetically, even only briefly. Instead of strategizing and fretting, attempt to relax your mind. Utilize a mantra such as "I'm handing over this difficulty to my guides to see what they can do."

6. Learn more about spirit guides.

Simply researching spirit guides will assist you in increasing your communication with them. Find uplifting, empowering, and healing expertise and information that speak to you.

Steps to take: Attend a workshop, enroll in an online class, or read a book about spirit guides, such as Angel Intuition, one of my most recent releases. Consider whether merely learning more about them opens the door to increased communication. Your guides will be ecstatic to have your undivided attention!

7. Strengthen your instincts.

Everyone possesses intuition, and everyone may develop it through study and practice. Indeed, there are four primary intuitive routes that you can experiment with and improve. (This intuition test can assist you in determining which is the strongest for you.)

For example, you can hear soothing voices in your head, see mental imagery, know breakthrough thoughts or mental downloads, or sense guidance in energy, emotions, and physical sensations (clairsentience).

Steps to take: Utilize your intuition to make little decisions that do not significantly impact, such as where to go for lunch with a coworker.

You can also engage in a game with your intuition by inquiring about which way to prioritize to communicate more effectively with your spirit guides. Inquire for a number between one and ten. Is there a particular number that stood out to you as you read this list? Did you hear, see, feel, or intuitively understand a particular number?

8. Establish spiritual practices daily, weekly, or monthly basis.

Spirit guides are from the spirit realm and possess an extraordinary capacity to anchor you in your spirituality or to assist you in discovering it. As a result of regular spiritual practices such as pulling an oracle card for inspiration in the morning, doing yoga, and attending spiritual gatherings with other people, you will develop a deeper connection with your spirit guides.

Take action in the coming weeks by performing a new moon or full moon ceremony to establish more consistent spiritual practices in your life.

Additionally, you can compose a list of some of your most significant spiritual beliefs, such as a strong belief that the Soul goes on after the body dies or a strong sense of connection to the Spirit whenever you spend time in nature.

9. Simply send a thought to your guides.

This may be the simplest and quickest method of connecting with your spirit guides, but it works. You can either offer a formal prayer or blessing or simply tell them what you need in a few quick sentences.

As soon as you've finished reading this section, ask your spirit guides for assistance with something you've been worried about in your thoughts. Then, enlist the assistance of a family member, coworker, expert, or health care professional. You are deserving of every available assistance!

10. Make use of a divination tool.

Humans have utilized divination tools to converse with Spirit for as long as they have existed. There are numerous divination tools available, including oracle cards, tarot cards, and runes. Experiment with various ways to determine which one works best for you.

Before working with your divination equipment, take a few deep breaths and close your eyes while holding whatever you're holding in your hands for a moment to center yourself. Then, discreetly request from your spirit guides that they deliver you a beneficial, healing message using this technology.

What to do if you feel you've lost contact with your spirit guides.

Do not be concerned if you feel disconnected from Spirit. You have always had a connection to Spirit. Your spirit guides are present, working behind the scenes on your behalf, whether you are aware of them. Even while we may feel disconnected from Spirit at some point in our lives, it is precisely at these moments when Spirit can and wishes to help us the most.

When you're going through a period of significant transition, it might be beneficial to reconnect with your spirituality and spirit guides. For example, watch a documentary or film with spiritual themes, listen to a podcast by a spiritual speaker who resonates with you, or spend 20 minutes each night before bed reading an uplifting and inclusive book about spirituality.

Your spirit guides aspire to have a more intimate relationship with you. As you become more receptive to and conversant with them, you may be pleasantly surprised by the number of messages you notice.

This is because your spirit guides already communicate with you regularly.

The invitation for the majority of people is to begin acknowledging the communication that is currently occurring.

Chapter 3

Ways To Honor Your Ancestors

We all have physical and spiritual ancestors, and each of our lives is founded on their sacrifice. They are as intimately connected to us as our breath and bones, and when consciously engaged, they can be an enormous source of healing, guidance, and friendship. Our chosen ancestors can include family members, friends, community members, religious and cultural leaders, and even non-human relatives like pets. In addition, our forefathers and mothers provide critical assistance in realizing our potential here on Earth while advancing their growth and maturation in the spirit realms through their involvement in our lives.

As with the living, deceased spirits range from intelligent and kind to self-absorbed and malevolent. Physical death is a significant event for the Soul, a rite of passage that we shall all experience. The living can provide essential momentum for the recently deceased to take the initiatory leap and become a beneficial ancestor. Once the deceased has been elevated to ancestors' status, part of their post-death journey may entail atoning for wrongs committed on Earth. It's beneficial to regularly spend time with our ancestors, both for their benefit and ours. The five suggestions below, which do not need belief in any particular religion or theology, are safe and practical methods to aid our cherished ancestors and welcome their continuous support and blessings in our daily lives.

As an Ethical and Loving Person, Fulfill Your Soul's Purpose

The most critical and most difficult way to commemorate our forefathers and mothers is to live up to our potential and life's purpose on Earth. Numerous cultures think that each has a unique destiny or karma to complete. Therefore, we should prioritize remembering these original instructions and doing what is necessary to express our gifts, real will, and most genuine selves. The ancestors are viewed as allies in this process of remembering and a source of strength and support to assist us in embodying our potential during this lifetime. But, on the other hand, if we are fortunate, our ancestors may bring about life changes that bring us back into contact with our Soul's longing and enhanced awareness of the agreements made before our birth.

While discussing destiny and calling is admirable, it is impossible to realize our greatest potential unless our lives and relationships are somewhat in order. For instance, learning solid ways of communicating feelings, subscribing to coming clean in your connections, looking for essential help for restraint and schooling, caring more for your body, and tolerating more noteworthy obligations regarding turning into an adoring and dependable individual are all important for the slow and ongoing course of turning out to be more aware individuals. Whatever assists us in developing into more ethical, balanced, and open-hearted individuals is one of the most powerful and honest tributes we can give to our forefathers and mothers.

Ironically, the exact things that would bring us down are frequently a legacy from our forefathers. Seeds of karmic dysfunction, such as alcoholism, patterns of abuse and dysfunction, religious extremism, sexism, wounds related to money or poverty, and a thousand and one other things can all be passed down through the bloodlines as seeds that can grow into full-blown dysfunction if watered properly. When properly comprehended, these difficulties may implicitly steer us toward the antidote, which is frequently a hidden internal resource that we also possess as a dormant ancestral inheritance. The gift of healthy warriors can be distorted by physical violence, scarcity anxiety can hide a wound in a family of strong providers, and addiction can dull the sensitivity needed by healers, artists, and lovers. These are just a few examples. In this sense, our forefathers and mothers can be both the source of difficulty and the remedy, but each time we make the correct choices in response to these inherited patterns, we elevate our own and their spirits.

Commit Beneficial Acts in the Name of the Ancestors

Almost all faiths recognize the spiritual reward of good deeds and giving. Charity in Christianity, sadaqah in Islam, tzedakah in Judaism, and dana in Buddhism and Hinduism are only a few religious expressions of a practically universal idea of practicing generosity and expressing our interconnectedness with and caring for others. Additionally, traditional, indigenous modes of life highlight the importance of sharing riches and the advantages of living a helpful, service-oriented existence. Mongolian shaman Sarangerel, a friend and instructor who died unexpectedly in 2006, half-jokingly defined shamanism as the science of designing Hinamori or "Windhorse," writing that This force is contained within the chest varies in size according to how it is used and accumulated. A powerful Windhorse enables the rider to think clearly and logically and see-through trickery. Windhorse is the force that enables shamans and other powerful people to perform tasks quickly and efficiently... Utilizing one's power for malicious purposes or to break the universe's balance depletes Windhorse... Windhorse can be increased through efforts to restore the universe's balance and religious practice.

Engaging in loving and truly beneficial deeds accumulates tangible and useful energy in the individual's energetic field or body. This can then provide a well-being that nourishes our soul, supporting the build of oneself into beneficial vessels. The impact of this can then lead us onto bigger, better, and greater outcomes.

The majority of individuals intuitively understand a similar principle: that the energetic impacts of actions can be directed or linked to persons who did not perform the actions. To illustrate, consider a private donation of ten million dollars in your name to help feed and house the homeless in your community. Contrast this to someone performing a private ritual in your name to consecrate an impending act of genocide; certainly less cool. But, in neither scenario, are you the one who does the activities? Family members giving charitable contributions in memory of a loved one who has passed away is an example of how this idea is already widely used.

Having a focused intention, engaging in meaningful activities, and personally connecting with the process of elevating the consciousness of your beloved deceased all contribute to the practice's success. For instance, if you feel that your grandmother's Spirit is disturbed or healthy and you wish to honor her life and Spirit, try dedicating a positive activity to her directly rather than to all your ancestors. The more focused the offering's goal, the more concentrated the impacts. Additionally, consider a service or action compatible with the recipient's individual life and Spirit.

For example, if your late father was a racist or committed domestic violence, you might donate to a charitable organization dedicated to racial healing or a shelter for survivors of women's domestic abuse. This can be two fold, in one way it may help to mitigate the harm caused by now changing to a more positive energy, and secondly all charity is helpful to the victims. Even though no abuse can be justified, one can only understand that the perpetrator may also have once been the victim of a similar abuse. Therefore, it's important as this also provides a recognition, repentance, confession or apology and now re-framing that negative low vibration into a positive high vibration for all..

Finally, setting a clear intention and emotionally connecting to the procedure will help ensure that the generated positive energy reaches its intended recipient.

While more involved acts of service are admirable, more straightforward commitments can be equally effective. Consider the following scenario: I had a frightening dream about my grandfather, who died last month, and I am left with the nagging suspicion that he has not yet entered the world of the ancestors. Later that morning, I'm at yoga class, where the teacher urges us to dedicate our yoga session to a specific intention. Recalling the dream, I pause and say softly to myself or loudly, "I dedicate the positive energy from this yoga session to my grandfather's well-being; may his spirit be at peace and united with our loving ancestors." Throughout the class, I keep him in my mind, visualizing him surrounded by love and light, reaffirming the connection between myself and the object of my prayer. Finally, after the class, I see a sphere of light, the Windhorse collected through this concentrated spiritual activity, enveloping the Spirit of my grandfather, bringing him happiness and well-being. Thus, I combine the strength of focused intent with the useful energy generated by a simple positive deed in a way that is beneficial and uplifting for the Spirit of my grandfather. The devotion of merit earned through little acts of kindness is a very useful practice for individuals who are unsure about the reality of their ancestors or who are not interested in direct spirit contact but wish to honor their loved ones' memories.

Continue to Be Receptive to Direct Communication from Your Ancestors

Direct communication with the spirits of one's ancestors can be fostered through ritual activities, but communication can also occur spontaneously through dream contact, waking experiences, and synchronicity. When we provide a framework for their outreach, their work becomes easier, and we become more receptive to the pleasures of conscious, ongoing engagement.

Speaking with or even listening to dead people, especially if they are your beloved dead folks, raises some eyebrows, and some of the fears may be justified. However, in terms of hearing voices, the experience of communicating with the deceased is usually never indicative of a psychotic state or disconnection from reality. If you or those close to you have any worries about whether you're coming apart, try seeking counseling from a grounded ancestor specialist, spiritually oriented psychotherapist, supportive mentor, or friend. The more typical worry is differentiating mental chatter from direct spirit contact, a refinement that I've discovered requires a good mix of faith and skepticism and time and effort.

Another critical consideration is to ensure that your interactions are primarily with loving, enlightened ancestors rather than conflicted or manipulative spirits. If you have spirit guides, ask them to provide a second opinion on the ancestors reaching you to ensure they are trustworthy. However, evolved and helpful forefathers and mothers may still lead with tough love and express themselves in boisterous and enigmatic ways, and it takes practice to distinguish the two again. Simply consulting your particular intuition is frequently sufficient to establish whether any spirit is fundamentally loving and well-intentioned. As a general rule, seek a second view if your relationship with an ancestor is not assisting you in becoming a more empowered, ethical, and loving person.

Dream Visitation

With a well-placed, emotionally packed dream, the ancestors may frequently reach even the most skeptical descendants. Not all dreams of the dead entail direct spirit contact. Determining whether an ancestor is attempting to communicate is not always straightforward; nonetheless, contact dreams are frequently accompanied by a felt experience of meeting the deceased loved one. Dreams about a deceased loved one's death may include getting a message or experiencing some healing. Suppose the dream has a contact quality and the departed appears to be in distress. In that case, you can send a direct prayer, healing rituals, and positive energy in their direction and happiness. If the ancestor appears to be in good spirits, merely being receptive to future dream contact and other relationship types facilitate future dream contact and other forms of relationship.

Waking Encounters

Even for those who do not believe in ghosts or seek touch with ancestors, the dead just come. They may occur during times of crisis or intensity, such as near-death experiences or four hours into a severe acid trip. Still, they occur more frequently in daily moments, such as while driving, lying in bed before sleep, or out walking the dog. These visits can be subtle at times, and if we are not vigilant, we might easily dismiss them as figments of our imagination or fantasy. For most people, these experiences are not visual and may not even be audio; instead, they are characterized by an awareness of someone being present for a brief moment, a direct knowing. For people who have a formal practice of ancestor veneration or a strong connection to the unseen worlds, such meetings may be quite common and are not necessarily charged with any more significance than a phone call from a friend. Even if we never seek direct communication from our beloved, simply having an open mind about the possibility of our beloved reaching us during our daily lives is a wonderful way to acknowledge our unbroken connection to our ancestors and the other world.

Synchronicity

Synchronicity, coined by Swiss psychologist Carl Jung, refers to two or more significantly connected events but is unlikely to occur otherwise. Although this is a difficult procedure to describe logically, the implication is that the ancestors may also communicate through occurrences. For example, assume your dead girlfriend adored lilacs, and you're on the front porch on the anniversary of her death, sipping a cocktail and feeling very depressed. At that point, your new neighbor approaches over to inform you that she is considering planting a lilac bush and requests your advice. You feel a chill run through your body and a sense that something amazing is taking place, that the worlds are temporarily colliding. You're left with the remarkable impression that your partner has reached out to console you after the chat. Significant radio tunes, written signs and messages, and unplanned animal encounters are just a few of the ways our forefathers brazenly exploited our environment to manufacture meaningful happenings and communicate their Message.

Establish a Physical Location to Pay Tribute to the Ancestors

I've frequently joked in my weekend ancestor training that if you don't have an ancestor altar, you become the altar. Having a space to pay tribute to the deceased can act as de-possession. The essential notion is abandoning an unconscious association with the ancestors favoring a relationship stance. When we designate a physical space to memorialize our forefathers and mothers, they become externalized, and their sanctified space serves as a reminder of the continuous relationship. The ancestral spirits can inhabit the physical location as a spirit house, sacred space, or inhabitation in this world. The crucifix, a statue of Krishna, or a copy of the Qur'an are all examples of objects that, through human understanding and, allegedly, the intervention of God or the gods, acquire a sacred significance.

The location and type of an ancestor-honoring spot might vary significantly according to tradition and individual preference. Cemeteries, tombs, shrines, and burial mounds all include human remains, which act as natural physical contact sites, much like a spirit house or energetic link to the deceased's Soul. Certain trees, mountains, rivers, and other natural elements may be culturally or personally associated with the ancestors as areas of heightened connection. Ancestor veneration may also occur in community temples and shrines, public monuments to the heroic dead, holy groves, and other ceremonial sites dedicated to working with the dead. The most frequent location for honoring the spirits of ancestors is likely the individual or family shrine, which is often located in or near one's home. By establishing an anchor for the ancestors' presence beyond our bodies and within the physical world, we externalize the deceased and establish circumstances for continued contact.

Suppose you feel inspired to create a personal ancestral altar in your house to strengthen your connection with your cherished ancestors; keep in mind that the shrine will ideally expand into a place where their energy can be more concentrated. As a result, you may wish to install the shrine in a location other than your bedroom, out of the way, or even enclosed, such as inside a cabinet, especially if you share your house with small children or boisterous dogs. The altar may take the form of a small table or shelf. It may contain photos of ancestors, stones, candles, vibrant fabrics, incense, inherited artifacts from the departed, inspired artwork, religious materials familiar to your ancestors such as a Bible or rosary, and other physical gifts. While some like to avoid images of the living on their ancestor shrines, and while I adhere to this rule, the essential thing is to enable the ancestors to direct you as to where and how their place of honor should be constructed.

After physically preparing the place of respect, I recommend a modest ceremony invoking the ancestors to activate and invigorate the shrine (for example, see the practice of "spirit feasting" below). Once engaged, the altar becomes a portal between worlds, a location of communication and enhanced connection with your beloved deceased. This is not to say that the ancestors reside exclusively at the shrine, any more than God resides exclusively in churches; rather, the altar serves as a dedicated, physical declaration of kinship with the ancestors. The process of responding to these relationships can then be amplified and deepened.

Take a few moments to tell the ancestors you no longer want to interact with the shrine, and then carefully undo what you've done, shutting the portal between the worlds that was opened by ritual action. If you have specific ancestor reverence traditions that inspire and instruct you on how to care for an ancestor shrine, that is fantastic; however, from my perspective, the only "right way" is whatever truly assists you in developing a sustained and heart-centered relationship with the ancestors your honor at your altar.

Make Offerings to the Ancestors

Human lovers typically value respect, passion, kindness, and quality time spent together. Plants thrive in a well-balanced environment with the sun, moisture, and healthy soil. While the Buddha appears to enjoy incense, the love goddesses may prefer honey, flowers, and all things sweet. Just as we nourish our human connections with specific forms of attention, involvement, and gifts, we may nourish our ancestral relationships via the practice of deliberate offerings. Acts of ceremonial feeding may emphasize a request we are making to our ancestors, express thanks for previously received assistance, or maintain the intimacy of an ongoing relationship.

Generally, it's prudent to decide the type of offering required initially. Next, please inquire about the offering's reception after presenting it and stating your goal. Finally, remain receptive to guidance or ripple effects such as intuitive communications, dream messages, or other ancestor indications. Food, drink, cash, cloth, tobacco, ash, tears, stones, other found objects, flowers, fire, and creations made with our hands are all physical gifts. Offerings to the ancestors can also take less human forms, such as singing, dance, prayer, healing and forgiveness practices, letting go of an unhealthy pattern or relationship, and undertaking obligations for personal or collective welfare.

One practice that exemplifies the importance of making sacrifices is the spiritual feast, or ritual meal, eaten with the ancestors. Once you've determined where you'll share this meal with your beloved departed (e.g., a special spot in nature, your ancestor shrine, or a cemetery) and the type of food and drink gifts they'd appreciate from you, you're ready to summon them. But, again, the only "correct" approach to invoke your forefathers and mothers is the one that works for you. Often, traditional approaches involve addressing them by name, passionate prayer, rattling, and heartfelt song. Unless you have additional experience with ancestor work, I recommend that you contact only the wealthy and supportive Dead; for the less fortunate, allow the helpful guides to pass the energy from any offerings to those in need.

Once you sense the presence of your loving and supportive ancestors, communicate with them and share the meal you've cooked with them by laying their food gift on your shrine, the Earth, or anywhere you've specified. Following the presentation of the offering, some traditions employ divination techniques to ascertain whether it was well-received and, if so, whether there are accompanying messages from the ancestors. Instead of a traditional divination procedure, simply take a moment to sense whether or not the food you cooked was welcomed. If something feels off, persevere with the process and be curious about what further may need to occur or be communicated. They may want a moment to savor what you've brought them or wish to transmit a wealth of information. Generally, it is beneficial to be receptive and curious after sacrificing the ancestors. After some time, typically at least a day, the food and drink offerings can be returned to the ground in the most environmentally conscious and attentive manner possible.

You do not need to be an indigenous shaman or a ghost whisperer to have a direct, intimate, and healthy relationship with your forefathers and mothers. However, because our ancestors care so much about our future generations' happiness and well-being, they are the ideal instructors for family healing, in my opinion.

Our ties to our forefathers and mothers require nurturing and regeneration, as with any significant relationship. By taking intentional steps to recognize and maintain these ties, our forefathers and mothers may become a wonderful source of healing, empowerment, and sustenance in our daily lives. Fortunately, these tending techniques are quite simple and may be performed by anyone with an earnest purpose.

Chapter 4

Using Your Higher Self To Receive Answers To Your Questions

The quickest way to true inner guidance is to learn the language of your Higher Self. Here are our top three ways to initiate communication with your Soul.

Have you ever met your Higher Self on a date?

The soul consciousness that is immeasurably more than the physical body you are familiar with is your Higher Self. Your Higher Self is the infinite and eternal 'you.' It is the aspect of you that inspires you, directs you through intuition, and instructs you through insight. Intentions, desires, and secrets are all fully known to your Higher Self. You are completely aware of yourself. However, you've had only a brief conversation with your Higher Self. If you allow this communication to thrive, those beneficial bursts of intuition and inspiration can become a larger part of your life.

Connecting with your Higher Self is a contradiction – you are constantly linked. Indeed, it is more than a link. It is unification. You cannot be divorced from your energetic consciousness-self on a physical level. However, we are here in this physical condition, which includes a sense of disconnection from everything else. There is no division in reality. Thus, where does your energy begin and end? This is how to establish contact with your Higher Self.

How Would You Describe Your Higher Consciousness?

Higher consciousness is a word that is frequently used to refer to a significant mental state that is relatively difficult to attain. It's a term frequently used by spiritual gurus, sages, and monks, and it's not always easy to define because human beings are intrinsically wired around main instincts.

Higher consciousness is often characterized as "the part of the human mind capable of transcending animal instincts," and lower consciousness is defined as "the part of the human mind capable of overcoming animal instincts."

Most of our waking hours are spent in semi-drowsiness, oblivious to anything but the immediate dangers around us—a byproduct of contemporary living.

Additionally, we believe that higher consciousness is an esoteric or religious concept rather than a scientific one. It might be seen as a popular concept of contemporary spirituality that seeks to demystify the concepts prevalent in old mystical teachings such as the Indian Vedas.

Nonetheless, human nature is not binary. On the contrary, its divine nature is embodied in the very name — a human being. "You are a human being," Ekhart Tolle, spiritual teacher, and the best-selling book emphasizes. When studied more closely, these two words explain who you are as a member of a certain species and speak to the dual aspect of your identity. Humanity is who you are physical: your body and mind. Your conditioned self is comprised of these two facets of your identity. That self is shaped by heredity and environment, and unknown elements. But, on the other hand, you are what you are because you are an unchanging, formless, and unconditioned consciousness. Assuming you take a gander at a wave or wave on an oceanside, you can't differentiate it from the sea or some other wave or wave, regardless of how comparable they show up on a superficial level."

How Can You Infuse Your Life With That Divine Essence?

In his book, The Spectrum of Consciousness, Ken Wilber, an American author of transpersonal psychology, uses lower and higher consciousness to describe the movement or evolution of human consciousness from personal to higher transpersonal consciousness.

When you rise beyond your own life and self-centeredness and focus on service to others, you ignite your divine nature from inside and become a better form of yourself. Is it feasible to gain access to a more evolved state of consciousness? Absolutely! With conscious attention, we can increase our frequency of access to higher consciousness, or the spiritual self, by becoming more focused on serving others than on serving ourselves.

What Is the Nature of Your Spiritual Self?

For a meaningful physical experience, your Higher Self is your best guide.

It is your intrinsic power to transcend time and overcome every obstacle.

Life's difficulties can serve as opportunities to reach a higher state of consciousness.— Tolle, Ekhart

According to Ekhart Tolle, those who believe that life exists to make them happy are in for a rude awakening. Every person on our Earth will face difficulties at some point. When you are eventually confronted with something heinous, you have a choice. You can feel depressed, bitter, furious, and unhappy. Alternatively, you can observe the unfolding problem from a more elevated state of consciousness and without judgment. Thus, your Higher Self is that capacity inside you that enables you to stay peacefully still in the face of any adversity. Additionally, your superior inner direction guides you toward the optimum course of action. Thus, whenever you experience an unexplained sensation of premonition, your Higher Self attempts to communicate with you.

What Is The Higher Self's Mode Of Communication?

If you've been brushing aside your intuition and gut sensations, you might want to consider why. Although the physical senses do not always detect information from the Higher Self, it is no less meaningful! After all, even though you cannot physically experience gravity, something prevents you from floating away like a birthday balloon. Many of us have grown accustomed to trusting in merely what our physical senses observe. As a result, we frequently overlook this vital component of ourselves — the energetic.

Another possible issue with the messages you receive from your Higher Self is that they are frequently jumbled, enigmatic, and completely perplexing, especially if they arrive in dreams.

It's quite beneficial to journal these enigmatic and symbolic messages since the answers frequently become apparent as you write about them. Occasionally, you will hear voices; at other times, you will receive visions or strong impulses to do – or not do – something.

One capacity that will emerge as you become accustomed to hearing your Higher Self is distinguishing between the ego's fear-based voice and the infinite/eternal voice of your Higher Self. You can cultivate an acute awareness of your body's capacity to serve as an excellent "translator" of your higher self's messages.

Three Methods For Connecting With Your Higher Self

1. Dreamland

To begin, your Higher Self communicates with you through your dream state — the subconscious domain. This is the state in which all mental constructs dissolve and seize control of your reality. For example, REM (rapid eye movement) sleep is characterized by the brain's neurons being just as active as they are while awake, yet your body is completely relaxed.

Most vividly remembered dreams occur during REM sleep when you connect with your higher consciousness. It is essential to remember and record your dreams to grow as a person.

Each night, your Higher Self communicates with you during your dream state to provide guidance and shine a light on your blind spots. Today's Message is to pay close attention to determine what you need to let go of at this point. It's critical to recognize that each figure in your dream represents a component of yourself — this or that subconscious aspect that you probably disavow. For instance, when you dream about a person who was formerly a part of your life, your Higher Self informs you that certain events occurred that you have not yet learned from. And now you're going to replicate those patterns.

Another example is how your Higher Self uses nightmare scenarios to attract attention to anxieties you need to release. Forgive yourself and others, or disavow your shadows, which emerge as persecutors or negatively charged figures in your dreams, depending on the symbolism of the nightmares you have. Once you master dream recall, you can master lucid dreaming and consciously connect with your Higher Self in lucid dreams.

2. Meditation

Meditation is one of the best techniques to build a direct connection with your Higher Self.

Your higher consciousness is not self-contained. It is perpetually present. The more elevated aspect of your consciousness has a high vibrational frequency. When you feel genuine love and thanks, and when you truly forgive, you live from your Higher Self consciousness. Thus, the meditation designed to assist you in connecting with your higher self is focused on boosting your vibratory frequency first and foremost.

You can either employ guided meditations or practice self-meditation by entering a profound state of gratitude for your life and then setting an intention to connect with your Higher Self.

Consider a serene, pleasant location, a place you enjoy being in. 'Do' in, not 'do' in. 'Be' included.

You can visualize your Higher Self as a physical presence, similar to your closest friend sitting by you. Alternatively, you can see yourself surrounded by a sea of warm, loving energy. Utilize whatever photographs are most appropriate for you!

Once you sense your Higher Self's presence, you can inquire about anything. The Higher Self is neither judgmental nor critical. Be receptive to all responses, regardless of their format.

Bear in mind that your responses may take the form of words, feelings, images, or sensations. Be receptive to whatever occurs. Keep a journal of anything online, as things may become evident after a while, either through synchronicities or dreams.

3. Intuitive Writing Or Journaling

You can pose questions and then scribble or type your initial, gut-reaction responses. Then re-read them while paying attention to your physical and emotional responses. You'll immediately discern whether your response came from the ego or the higher self. Additionally, journaling assists in making meaning of messages that you do not immediately "understand." If the replies appear to be smarter than usual, this is the work of the higher self. If your responses sound forced or as if you're telling other people what they want to hear, they're coming from the ego.

How Do I Distinguish Between My Ego And My Higher Self?

Thus, how can you discern between a fear-based response from your ego and the voice of your Higher Self?

How do you know the responses aren't a figment of your imagination or something your mind concocted to appease you?

This is how:

If you are experiencing physical symptoms of anxiety, tension, fear, or anger, you communicate with your ego.

The ego constructs its identity in response to pain.

That is what it is aware of. That is the environment in which it is at ease and the language in which it communicates. It desires to remain identified with that negativity to maintain an identity.

When you experience physical sensations of lightness, love, energy, or happiness, you communicate with your Higher Self.

The Higher Self lacks identity. It is simply energy, without beginning or end. The Higher Self's natural condition is freedom, love, and joy.

One strategy is to ask yes/no questions and then listen for an immediate response – often even before the question is finished.

This quick answer is most likely coming from your Higher Self, bypassing the mind's training. If you allow yourself time to study your question, believe me, when the ego will immediately begin its typical negative commentary!

Your best guidance is you — that is, the higher you.

Your supreme educator.

Therefore, schedule a meeting with your higher self and discover what is going on in your life. Pose significant questions from the perspective of your "great self."

Your life will take on a new meaning – and potentially a new direction – as your higher self guides you in the best way for you.

Chapter 5

Effective Ways To Connect
With Your Ancestors

Your forefathers and mothers are present. That has always
been the case, and it will continue to be so in the future.
When you take a breath, you're using your ancestral DNA.
When you cry or laugh, you do it with the DNA of your forefathers
and/or mothers. I've spent the last five years connecting in various
ways with my ancestors. There are a few books available to assist you
in your endeavors. However, this is something I had to learn on my
own. Now I wish to share my experiences with you to assist you in
developing a stronger connection with your ancestors and help them
become a pillar of your spiritual practice.

Cultural Ties and Ancestors

For thousands of years, ancestor worship has been an integral aspect
of spiritual practice worldwide. However, with the advent of
Abrahamic religions, ancestor worship virtually vanished. This
religious evolution has caused us to forget our forefathers and mothers
and, therefore, our origins. This is a regrettable step in the wrong

direction. By losing contact with our forefathers and mothers, we lose touch with our roots...with the blood that flows through our veins. The Chinese, Native Americans, ancient Egyptians, ancient Romans, numerous African tribes, and Indians are just a few societies that pay tribute to their ancestors. So why have we abandoned ancestral worship? How do we re-establish contact with long-forgotten ancestors?

Methods for Establishing Contact With Your Ancestors

- genealogy
- scrapbooking
- genealogy

1. Genealogy

The first step toward connecting with your ancestors is to become acquainted with them. That sounds difficult, given their demise, doesn't it? Wrong! Even though it's a lot of work, it's worth it in the long run. Create a family tree online, in a Word document, or by hand. For myself, I used ancestry.com's online family tree. The nice thing about ancestry.com is that it does information searches across a massive database of files and documents. If you enter your parents' names first, the system will instantly notify you of document matches. For instance, you might come upon your father's war records or an article about your mother. These are merely illustrative examples.

More on Family Trees

Creating a family tree is to learn about your forefathers and mothers in terms of their names, the periods in which they lived, their jobs, the places they resided, and their origins. In the United States, if you don't have Native American Ancestry, your ancestors came from somewhere else (obviously). Are you familiar with their ancestors' homeland? Are you familiar with the traditions, beliefs, and history of the land of your forefathers and mothers? These are all excellent ways to go into your lineage and learn about your forefathers and mothers.

DNA and Ancient Ancestors

Getting one's DNA tested is a little nerve-wracking for some people. I've had mine done, and it's aided me in numerous ways in reconnecting with my relatives... However, for some the downside could be revealing. Therefore, be aware of the possible realizations and what consequences of DNA testing might bring to one knowing your lineage is a mix of various countries and cultures. However, after analyzing your DNA, you may be joyful to learn about your ancestral links.

Along with DNA testing through Ancestry or 23andMe, upload your results to MyTrueAncestry to learn about your ancient and medieval relatives! For instance, my original DNA findings indicated that I am half English... However, MyTrueAncestry determined that I am a Saxon, Celt, and Danish Viking!

2. Scrapbooking

Create a scrapbook of your ancestors once you've constructed a family tree. This is another time-consuming project; nevertheless, by focusing on their lives, you will get closer to them. Collect stickers, craft sheets, media, and any other morsels you wish to include in a huge scrapbook purchased from a craft store. Keep this book exclusively for your ancestors. From there, begin by sorting your ancestors alphabetically or by family name, whichever you prefer. Then include photographs of your forefathers and mothers, their names, dates of birth and death, and jobs. Anything that you believe is significant and pertinent to your relationship with your ancestors can be included in the book.

Shutterfly

If you're not crafty, Shutterfly.com can create a scrapbook for you. I've used this service numerous times to create beautiful photo albums commemorating family vacations and holidays. I recently assembled a whole album of my grandmother's ancestors as a gift for her. Following that, I knew my forefathers and mothers were delighted and honored. It costs between $30 and $60, depending on the number of images you want in your album. However, it takes care of the physical labor for you!

Framing Photos

Along with ancestor scrapbooking, it's time to frame any older photographs of your relatives (particularly originals). The time you spend framing and hanging these photographs is time spent with your ancestors. Consider them and their lives and the blood that rushes through your veins and how it also did so in theirs. Hang these images in a single location to honor your forefathers and mothers, or distribute them throughout the house to demonstrate reverence and summon protection over your household.

Ways to Develop a Spiritual Bond with Your Ancestors

- altars
- offerings

- dreamwork

- ritual

- prayer

- hobbies

- altars

3. Construct Ancestral Altars

You've spent time learning about your forefathers' and mothers' life; now it's time to connect with them spiritually. First, make a place of worship for your ancestors, such as an altar or a shrine. Inside or outside, the altar can be placed. It might be a single hallway corner or a complete wall in your living room. Candles, photos, mementos/heirlooms, flowers, herbs and stones, and incense are essential elements to add to your ancestor's altar.

4. Ancestor Offerings

After establishing your ancestral altar:

1. Continue honoring them with an offering.

2. When selecting an offering, ensure that your forefathers and mothers enjoy it.

3. If you're commemorating ancient ancestors, make an educated guess.

They will notify you if something is wrong...trust me. Springwater, wine/mead/beer, various fruits (apples and citrus fruits store well on an altar for days), cakes and bread, cigars, and tobacco are all examples of ancestral offerings. Replace them as necessary.

5. Dreamwork

Our forefathers and mothers will visit us in our dreams. How do you effortlessly communicate with and connect with your ancestors? Invite your ancestors to pay you a visit in your dreams. You'll be amazed at how rapidly they appear. I had a dream visit from a certain ancestor, and I remembered her name. Before I learned, she was an ancestor, and it wasn't until I began researching the family tree that I realized she was! I initially misread one of the letters in her name, but she made it perfectly obvious later on! You should simply request that they appear. Make a note of your ancestor's dreams in the morning so you can refer to them later.

6. Ritual

Include your forefathers and mothers in your rituals and meditations. Solicit the protection of your circle and workings from your ancestors and invite them to be present. First, I recommend welcoming them to your sacred area and asking for favors. With the mere purpose of connecting with your ancestors, you can develop an entire ritual. While some people are adept at creating their rituals, if you are not one of them, here is one of mine.

7. Ancestor Prayer

When I pray, I rarely address my prayers to God or Goddess...

I offer prayers to my forefathers and mothers. Communicate with them as if they are standing next to you, listening to every word you say. I do this either silently or aloud, depending on who is there. You might also pray to your forefathers and mothers. It doesn't need to be ornate or rhyme. You are not required to bow or get down on your knees. They are a part of your family and wish to hear from you. Simply pray.

8. Hobbies

A powerful technique to learn how to connect with your ancestors is to replicate their actions. For example, was your granny a crocheter? It's time to grab the crochet needle! Was your great-grandfather an accomplished fly fisher? Consider picking up his hobby. Alternatively, go back in time and acquire a skill that your forefathers and mothers may have possessed: survival skills such as fire building, hunting, and weaving.

9. Foods

Cooking meals in honor of your ancestors is a pleasant way to connect, especially if you enjoy eating. Make the bread pudding from your grandmother's recipe or the gingerbread from your aunt's recipe. Recreate a recipe from one of your family's old cookbooks. OR conduct a study on the foods consumed by your forefathers and mothers in their ancestral homeland. For instance, if your ancestors were Irish, you might want to try Dublin coddle, soda bread, or colcannon. If the guests are Nigerian, they should order pepper soup, gari, or egusi soup. Make a place for your ancestors at the table and put a portion of the food on their altar.

10. Meditation

In addition to being beneficial in various ways, meditation can also be utilized to communicate with your ancestors. On YouTube, look for a guided meditation. Wait till you have a peaceful minute to yourself. Switch off all electronic devices and dim the lights. Solicit the presence of your ancestors and the presence of your ancestral guide during your meditation. Then allow them to communicate with you in that calm area.

How To Make A Personal Connection With Your Ancestors

These days, a common question is better connecting with one's ancestors.

Why is it important for me to feel connected to the cultures of my ancestors and grandmothers? How can I translate the results of an ancestry test into genuine wisdom? How do I trace my ancestors' tribal ties beyond modern-day national boundaries? How do I get beyond the repeated consumer culture of material I'm told?

I adore these inquiries.

Not because I own all the answers, but because I am a participant in this investigation alongside you all. After a year of hard research and instruction from my teacher and listening and dreaming, I've realized that I've just scratched the surface.

As a result, I've set aside my inner perfectionist (the one who requires immediate knowledge of all the solutions) and welcomed this lifelong journey back to my roots.

Because reconnecting with your ancestral Ancestry is remembering your place in the world.

It's how you reconnect with yourself, independent of any societal norm, body shape, religion, or tribal clique.

When you realize that you belong here on Earth, that a deep and powerful wildness is stirring within you, and that your ancestors'

DNA still resides in your cells, a great deal of that profound need to feel at home begins to dissolve.

Before I go into what has worked for me, I want to establish some ground rules here.

This will not be an easy path to the promised land.

Human history has been fraught and complicated by migrations, wars, famines, family separations, and traumas, to name a few. Over the ages, many knowledge and authentic accounts of history have been lost (not just the ones we read in school - the ones written by the winners).

What makes this research so compelling and delightful is framing it as a lifelong treasure hunt, in which pieces of the puzzle reveal themselves as you progress from one hint to the next.

A Guide for Reconnecting with Your Ancestral Lineage

1. Get the DNA test

To begin, I strongly advise you to have a DNA test. It was quite beneficial in clearing any stories or assumptions I had about being a quarter of this or two-fifths of that.

Seeing the spread of various European areas discovered through my DNA helped me see how my ancestors traveled from Scandinavia's northern territories down through the British Isles. In contrast, others went inland to modern-day France and Germany. The test taught me that national identity is a recent idea in human history. My ancestors traveled around (due to food sources, weather, availability of water, conflict, and falling in love, among other factors) to form the vast tapestry of my ancestral background.

My favorite part of the entire procedure was connecting with my grandmothers, first and foremost, via my maternal haplogroup.

There are disputes over whose company is better, 23andMe, Ancestry DNA, or National Geographic, and I have no opinion. I chose 23andMe because they offered a sale, and I desired raw genetic data for health grounds. I've heard that while 23andMe makes it easier to hunt down your maternal haplogroup than Genealogy does, Ancestry provides a prettier interface for genetic Ancestry. Follow your intuition.

It's better to take DNA results with a grain of salt, as they are not always correct. To understand what I mean, read this chapter and keep in mind that these tests do not determine your DNA's origins in the past, but rather the location of your DNA on Earth today.

2. Familiarize yourself with the history and geography of your ancestral homelands

Pick one place and dig in to learn more about it as soon as you know where your ancestors originated.

Read up on the history of those locations to better understand who ruled when. Determine the dates of key wars, famines, and the advent of industrialization. Was it previously engulfed by a colossal boreal forest or an ice sheet?

The more you learn about the land's history and terrain, the easier it will be to imagine what your ancestors went through.

And when I refer to "the land," I want you to be as specific as possible. Rather than focusing on Italy as a whole, check if you can narrow your search to a certain village or set of cities. Your ability to connect with the lives of your ancestors who lived in a particular bioregion will be enhanced if you can recognize it with its lakes, mountains, and valleys.

3. Find out what your ancestors have to say about it.

I understand if this is impossible for any of you because of adoptions, death, or a wish to withdraw from family for mental health and well-being actively. If that describes you, you may skip this part, knowing that there are still other opportunities to connect with your family., this isn't the only choice available.

However, if you have access to family stories (through conversations with family members or written recollections from your genealogy-obsessed Great Uncle), devise a strategy for obtaining them. Take a recording of a chat you have with your grandmother. Create duplicates of ancient diaries. Make time and space to absorb these tales and imprint them on your heart.

We live in such a fast-paced and connected world that many of us forget to print the photo memories we share on our social media accounts every week (Note: print your photos!). Our stories have been forgotten because the documents were destroyed, the people who knew them best passed away, or no one took the time to document them.

Therefore, save some room on your next trip home or family reunion. Then, the picture will be painted for your story by story, little by bit.

4. Conduct a public records search

We live in an era when we may access a wealth of information and gems about our ancestors via digitized public documents. You might begin by registering for a free trial account on Ancestry.com and conducting research there.

It's not all bad news, though. Many free resources, like your local library and the Mormon church, are available. True, the Mormon church maintains highly extensive genealogical records accessible to anyone.

5. Build an Ancestor Altar

Now we're going to talk about more magical and energetic tools—the stuff that's changed my life.

Create an altar to your ancestors to focus your intentions and invite them into your place.

This might look like anything, so avoid getting too caught up in how it's supposed to look or how many embellishments you add. I like to begin by placing any artifacts that belonged to my forefathers and mothers on it and photographs. Then I use small things from nature that capture the essence of the season (since our forefathers were more seasonal than we are today) and anything else that speaks to me.

My altar is where I spend the majority of my time each week. I can see it from my desk at my office, which is situated next to a window. I light a candle and pronounce my ancestors' names out, expressing appreciation, requesting protection, and only good intentions (especially considering a few ancestors with whom I'd prefer to avoid having a relationship). Sometimes, I rearrange the altar. On other days, I scarcely notice. This devotional practice of using an altar to connect more deeply with your ancestors can be quite powerful. Try that and see what happens.

6. Establish a Dream Practice to Establish a Connection with Your Ancestors

The dream realm can be a powerful source of medicine for our waking existence.

We consult dream dictionaries and speak with therapists about our dreams even in our ultra-western and skeptical world. The dream environment contains a great deal of magic, which we may use to connect more profoundly with our desires and heal past wounds. Dream space is a site of regenerative creativity nourished by waking life and then my dream life, each of which serves the other indefinitely.

In our forefathers' time, dreams were a means of divining truth, connecting with spirit, and navigating the maze of existence. In many traditions, a group would appoint a respected elder to facilitate meaningful ties with their dream time.

I ask you to create a practice of Dreamtime communication with your ancestors. Your practice might be as simple as establishing an intention or asking a question shortly before bed. "I need the guidance of my matrilineal line to overcome this cycle that keeps repeating in my waking life," or simply, "Will my ancestors make themselves known to me?" are all possible requests.

This technique involves patience, curiosity, and the discipline to write down or record your dreams immediately upon waking. The messages will unfold over time as you record and pay attention to your dreams.

7. Establish a connection with your People's Folkways

For me, remembering is a sensory experience.

I lack a sense of my roots due to extensive cerebral book research. That portion is beneficial, but when I combine it with my other senses, my feelings of a profound recall are truly aroused.

When I say "incorporating my senses," I mean eating the food that my ancestors prepared, listening to their folk songs (there are some excellently curated playlists on Spotify), watching and learning their folk dances (for example, the Polish polka or the Italian tarantella), and reading or listening to the ancient myths and folktales that have endured over time.

It is critical to connect with your people's folkways since they are the traditions that have endured the rise of the Empire over generations and throughout the world. These are the means through which our ancestors were not colonized.

8. Make a Pilgrimage to Your Ancestors

If it is truly feasible for you, I firmly instruct you to visit the terrains concerning your kin and truly contact the dirt, drink the water, eat the food, and inhale the air.

Conduct preliminary research to ensure that you visit sites significant to your ancient ancestors, such as holy wells, sacred burial sites, and gathering spots. Request permission to visit the village where one of your ancestors was born. Determine their location and visit them to express gratitude and honor.

As someone who has recently visited one of the numerous ancestral homelands, I can confidently state that physically being on ancestral grounds creates an incredible depth of connection. In Ireland, every stone I stepped on brought me back to a period long ago. While sipping a strong cup of tea served by my Airbnb host, I sipped cider at an 800-year-old pub and looked out over the misty hills. I won't forget it for the rest of my life.

Ancestral Connection through Food

For as long as I can remember, I've been interested in food as a cultural and personal expression. Food can express so much—not simply a desire to connect with family and friends, but also as a barometer of what is occurring on the land and in your community.

Your family is likely to have its cooking traditions.

My Italian friends always eat cioppino (fish stew) on the eve before Christmas. My family eats smoked salmon to honor our Scottish ancestors on Christmas morning. My friend's grandfather adored boxed confetti cake to the point where they now serve it at every family function.

When I speak with women about reconnecting with their ancestors, many lose where to begin. It's overwhelming—even more so if they're not particularly connected to their own family.

As an answer to them (and to you), I suggest that you think about the diet of your people. Once you've identified your group (which may be numerous—I am descended from several tribes and European nationalities), pick one, to begin with, and conduct research on the foods they ate. I enjoy poring over old folk stories and mythology from my people to discover what foods are referenced. After all, our forefathers and mothers required food as well. But, what type of food did they cultivate? When and how did they collect their food?

Keep an open mind and inquire of Grandmother Google what she has to share with you.

I was invited to an ancestral potluck last spring, where we were each required to bring food from our tribe (such an incredible idea, by the way...

It's an excellent opportunity to engage with and learn about your community, and it's also rather tasty).

While preparing for the potluck, I researched ancient Scottish lore and came upon the selkie legends.

Selkies are fabled merfolk who can walk on land after shedding their seal skins. Selkie sightings (and even falling in love with them) originated in Scotland's fishing culture—lonely fishermen telling tales of witnessing a seal lose her skin and transform into a lovely woman right before their eyes.

My favorite part of learning about the selkies was how they ate Scotch eggs, which were hard-boiled eggs rolled in sausage meat and baked in breadcrumbs. As a result, I baked falafel-coated scotch eggs and took them to the potluck, along with stories about the selkies.

This week, I've been reeling from a strong ancestral connection to soup—specifically, lima bean soup.

After months of begging, my mother handed off a whole grocery bag loaded with descriptions of my ancestral history on both sides of my family. These books and files contain a wealth of information about those who came before me. I am indebted to my mum and relatives who felt compelled to document and collect my people's stories. At least not everyone has the same level of knowledge that I have.

A diary entry detailing my great-grandmother Philomena's life as a poor immigrant family from Poland in the early 1900s was discovered while sifting through the barely legible handwritten records of ships built in Maine in the 1600s and marriages, births, and deaths in the state. She penned it with the help of her younger sister, Elizabeth.

They had a very terrible time of it back then.

The four young children worked in a shrimp factory in New Orleans to pay for their mother's one-bedroom factory apartment. These were the days before child labor restrictions (and compulsory education), and they were eking out an existence. My great-grandmother was six years old.

The majority of the diary entries addressed the family's living situation and what kept them going throughout the day. It brought back memories of how they formed a line to get their turn to rock in the rocking chair as soon as they awoke and how she had to travel back and forth across the floor of their home late at night, cradling her baby brother in her arms, so their mother could sleep.

However, the passage about lima bean soup jumped out to me.

While her father was gone on business, Philomena lived with her mother, and four siblings caught fire.

Dear Reader,

As independent authors it's often difficult to gather reviews compared with much bigger publishers.

Therefore, please leave a review on the platform where you bought this book.

Many thanks,

Author Team

Want Free New Book Launches?

Email "Ancestral Veneration" at:

mindsetmastership@gmail.com

Chapter 6

African Ancestors

A frican forefathers and mothers provide Africans with a common and personal feeling of self-affirmation, identity, and unrestricted belonging. No wonder Mazisi Kunene, the famed Zulu poet, is renowned for his epic Shaka the Great and another magnificent poetry collection, Ancestors and the Sacred Mountain. The ancestors play a significant role in African literature, from Chinua Achebe's classic Things Fall Apart through Ola Rotimi's The Gods Are Not to Blame and AC Jordan's The Wrath of the Ancestors. There is little doubt that travels to areas of Africa such as Gorée in Senegal and Elmina in Ghana, which was the epicenters of the transatlantic slave trade, can serve as a means of conjuring the world of African ancestors, albeit through traumatic recollection and remembering.

The island of Gorée should now be a UNESCO World Heritage Site off the coast of Senegal, opposite Dakar. Touring Gorée, once the world's largest slave trade port, contributes to humanity's goal of "never again" experiencing such a horrific experience, as the legendary Nelson Mandela taught us all.

To this day, kingdoms such as the Ashanti in Ghana and the Zulu in South Africa continue to be critical touchstones in the history of Africans and their reverence for their forefathers. In the songs of Mali's famous griots, Fela Kuti's rebellious Afrobeat sounds, Congolese soukous sounds, and Southern African migration ballads, ancestors are unapologetically and deeply invoked. How could anyone forget South African Hugh Masekela's enduring classic, Stimela?

Even though many Africans have embraced religions not indigenous to Africa in recent centuries, Africans still place a high premium on ancestors. Although Christianity and Islam are the most prevalent religions in Africa today, ancestors remain significant to most Africans. This is not because Africans are inferior to God's children. Africans' continued growth can be attributed to their strong ancestors and spirits, which powerful ancestral protectors have guarded. Without African forebears, the concept of Africa and Africans is unimaginable.

It is not hyperbole to assert that African forefathers have obstinately maintained Africa and the African Diaspora as powerful globally. As a result, Africans are establishing a foothold in the world. African forefathers affirm unequivocally and unequivocally that Africans are not descendants of bastard trees. They help educate the African youngster about the dangers of fire and water from an early age. They instill a sense of responsibility for something greater and more meaningful than worldly gain.

Without a sense of debt and humble submission to the ancestors' wishes and guidance, most Africans feel lost and are frequently compelled to do numerous rituals to satisfy their ancestors. Any

African who sincerely loves life balance dreads the wrath of their forefathers and seeks to honor them constantly.

When Africans commemorate the existence of their forefathers and mothers, they commemorate a significant and beloved history. They are defending the strength of their indigenous spirituality and their profound ties to the land they have lost or may still possess. Through oral tradition, each family member is generally informed about their forefathers and mothers—another significant component of the African experience. When Africans butcher beasts in traditional rites, they communicate with their ancestors, and the family leader would frequently repeat the names of that family's ancestral line. Without a written record, this calling of the ancestors assists in transmitting essential knowledge and family-specific rites and customs. When kids are told about their ancestors, it is frequently done by individuals who are invested in their family's heritage and who believe in the cyclical nature of spiritual existence.

Africans are proud of their forebears, driven by a sense of purpose, and respectful toward life in all its forms, past, present, and future. Ancestors are eternally alive in the African world and cosmological concept of existence in the African world. Africans' ancestors establish connections with their loved ones, bless their fertility celebrations, and intercede when spiritual impediments and contaminating factors threaten order, happiness, health, and life. Africans invoke their ancestors when life's thunderstorms threaten to envelop and even destroy them. Without the invocation of ancestors, complete metaphysical harmony is unachievable for most Africans. Belief in ancestors is a basic aspect of African identity. That has always been the case. And may it remain so in perpetuity. Between Cape Town and Cairo. Between Morocco and Madagascar. Long live African forefathers and mothers!

Ways to Pay Tribute to the Ancestors

To honor your forefathers and moms, now may be the best moment to get started. (However, you do not require an occasion to pay them homage and express gratitude for their direction and protection.)

Even if you don't realize it, you already have a connection to your ancestors and mothers. Your generational ties were formed long before anyone died (and before you were born). Consequently, you may find yourself drawn to family customs and hobbies or develop a tendency to side-eye people the way your great-auntie used to do." While the tie remains, creating or re-forming relationships with ancestors allows you to acknowledge them, invite them to walk beside you, and express thanks for their presence in your life. (Gratitude is the operative word here—please refrain from requesting favors and blessings until you have formed relationships and expressed gratitude.)

Before we begin, it's important to understand that not every ancestor is amenable to cooperating with you (and you might not be open to working with them). Generational trauma is real, and we know that not everyone — including some family members — has your best interests at heart. For instance, some Black people may have oppressive white ancestors, while others may have abusive white forebears. Certain ancestors may not want to be disturbed. When connecting with your ancestors, use your intuition and judgment. After all, they are spirits, and dealing with spirits should not be treated lightly.

If you're new to ancestral veneration, we recommend beginning with ancestors with whom you had a trusted relationship on this level, such as a deceased grandfather or uncle. Additionally, you can pronounce protection mantras before particular rites to invite only the presence of benevolent ancestors. "Ancestors who advise and adore me" and "Ancestors who are here for my highest good" are two of our favorites.

Now that we've established that, here are some basic methods you can embrace and adapt to elevate your forefathers and mothers:

Preserve Their Final Resting Places

Visiting and preserving resting places is a straightforward yet significant method to pay tribute to recent ancestors. While most of you are probably already doing this, it does not have to be limited to specific dates such as birthdays or anniversaries. Make it a point to visit and tidy your deceased loved ones' gravesites regularly. Decorate their resting places with flowers or their favorite objects. Spend meaningful time with them while you're there. Were they bibliophiles? Read a few chapters of a book you believe they will enjoy. Were they constantly dancing? While cleaning their space, play music. With physical and emotional offers, make your time with them exceptional.

P.S. This also applies to non-burial forebears. If you know where their remains are, go there and establish touch with them.

Establish An Altar

Create a sacred area on your shrine for your ancestors and ancestral ceremonies. If you already have an altar, you can embellish it with some of your loved ones' possessions, items that remind you of them, or their photographs. (You may also include photographs of community forebears who have inspired you, such as Toni Morrison, Harriet Tubman, or Nina Simone.) Even better, you can dedicate an altar to your forefathers and mothers.

Additionally, you can use your altar to make offerings. For instance, you may set a glass of one of your ancestor's favorite beverages or fresh flowers on your shrine in their honor. On the birthdays of my ancestors, I like to light white candles on my altar. As always, remember to maintain and care for your assigned place for them.

Offer Libations

You've offered libations if you've ever "poured one out" for a deceased friend or family member. (Notice how deeply ingrained our roots are? Without recognizing it, some of us have engaged in ancient rites). Typically, we honor the memory of loved ones by providing offerings to the spirits, but other sacred offerings like tea or water may also be offered.

Offering libations can be a full-fledged ceremony or as simple as saying a message or praying for your ancestor and then pouring your libation into the Earth. This could be their burial, a plant, or an outdoor sacred location.

When my great-grandmother died last month, I said a prayer to thank her for her life and bless her transition to the next level before pouring water into a tree she directed me to. Nothing extravagant but lovely (and she acknowledged, accepted, and thanked me for my offering a couple of days later).

Simply Connect

Often, the most meaningful approach to honor your forefathers and mothers is to just make room for them. Prayer, meditation, and writing are excellent ways to communicate with your ancestors. You can even inquire as to how they wish to communicate with you. Because several of my ancestors indicated that they like to communicate with me through tarot and meditation, I make time for them through those disciplines. Perhaps one of your ancestors enjoyed fishing; therefore, a wonderful method to spend time with them is to sit alone on the dock to connect with their spirit.

All of the ancestors you work with will communicate differently, so pay attention to their cues and make time to maintain the unique connections just as you would if they were physically present—because they are!

Chapter 7

Locating Your Biological Family

1. Participate in an AncestryDNA® test.

Taking an AncestryDNA® test is one of the most effective ways to locate your biological family members. Even if the individual you're looking for has not taken the test, a close relative may have. The good news is that DNA testing is gaining popularity; there are presently 20 million persons in the AncestryDNA database (and counting).

Your Ancestry® account will be the only place you'll be able to see your findings once they're ready. While you wait for results, begin creating a family tree and recording your biological ancestors. Then, once you've obtained your DNA findings, incorporate them into your tree.

2. Examine your most recent DNA matches.

Click View All DNA Matches from your DNA homepage to view a list of your biological relatives who have done the AncestryDNA test.

Your matches are sorted according to the amount of DNA you share; the higher a match ranks on your list, the more closely related you are. If you haven't found a nearly related match yet, have no fear; your list of matches is constantly updated.

Begin by examining the closest match and their family trees. You'll see the number of persons in your matches' trees if they have public, linked family trees. If their tree is green, it is considered public property. If it is gray, they either have a private tree or none. A lock indicates that the tree is secure. A green leaf indicates the discovery of a common ancestor. If you're interested in viewing a match's private tree, ask if they're prepared to share it with you.

3. Contact your matches.

Select a name from your list of DNA matches and then click Message. Introduce yourself and explain that you are seeking a biological family member. Because your Message may come as a surprise, it's prudent to consider probable family dynamics—the Barefoot Genealogist at Ancestry shares some insights into how she dealt with her surprise AncestryDNA matches. Because not everyone reads their Ancestry messages consistently, please check back for a response.

4. View your shared matches.

Select a name from your list of DNA matches, then select the Shared Matches tab to view a list of matches that you and that match share. Examine the family trees of your shared matches for shared surnames, locations, and specific persons. If you have a first cousin match who does not have a tree, consider contacting them and collaborating on one. If you discover an ancestor who appears in the trees of at least two of your common matches, you've discovered someone to research.

5. Look for common ancestors.

When you discover the name of a prospective ancestor, determine their relationship to you. Utilize the projected relationship to infer the generation of an ancestor in the tree you generated; for instance, a shared ancestor with a second cousin could be your great-grandparent. Enter the ancestor in any of your tree's great-grandparent slots—it makes no difference which one. You can reposition them once you've determined their proper placement.

6. Start descendancy research.

When you find an ancestor, identify each of their children, grandchildren, great-grandchildren, and great-great-grandchildren, all the way up to the present. At this point, even ambiguous, non-identifying information from your adoption files or your adopted parents can be beneficial. Utilize Ancestry trees, obituaries, and online directories to piece together your family's unknown ancestors.

7. Contact living family members.

You may discover probable grandparents, aunts, uncles, cousins, siblings, and parents while tracing your family. Even if you're unsure about your relationship, contacting these individuals may help you fill in the gaps. After they've listened to your narrative and absorbed the facts, you can measure their enthusiasm in doing a DNA test to validate your suspicions.

8. Consult a professional.

Consider employing experienced researchers if you run into a brick wall. Ancestry ProGenealogists® has a long history of assisting individuals in conducting biological family research. Our genetic research packages combine DNA evidence with traditional genealogical research to help you locate long-lost family members. Pricing begins at $3,900.

Inspiring Ways to Connect
with Your Family's History

More than names and dates, family history is about connection.

You are descended from millions of forefathers and mothers. And you may not know who they are at the moment, or they may be just names with dates to you. However, one of the joys of family history is the opportunity to connect with these ancestors and produce artifacts that will allow future generations to connect with both you and them. So here are some suggestions to get you started.

1. Maintain a diary of your life. It may be a handwritten journal, a blog, a digital scrapbook, a photo journal, or a collection of audio recordings—the possibilities are endless!

2. Locate the graves of your forefathers and mothers. You can visit a cemetery or search online for images of headstones. Numerous websites host databases of headstone images. If you visit a cemetery, you may like to photograph headstones and submit them to these websites so that others may view them.

3. Pay a visit to sites that are meaningful to your family. Take photographs of those locations and document the events that occurred there. Consider requesting a tour of a relative's hometown from a relative. Alternatively, take a tour of your own home and neighborhood. Again, take photographs of the tours for posterity!

4. Gain a better understanding of your forefathers' and mothers' festivities. Investigate the holidays your forefathers and

mothers would have observed and how they observed them in their place and period. Then observe their holidays appropriately or adopt their customs into your own.

5. Keep photographs. Take new photographs, collect old ones, and then preserve them for future generations. Ensure that they are labeled with names so that individuals may be identified. At FamilySearch.org (click on "Images"), you'll find an excellent facility for uploading, storing, and sharing photos.

6. Host an indexing celebration. If you need help indexing at FamilySearch.org/indexing, invite friends and family over to your place.

7. Reenact a story from your family's history. For family home evening, recreate an event from your family's past. This is an enjoyable approach to educating younger siblings about their family history.

8. Write down what you wish you knew about your great-grandparents about yourself. Next, consider five inquiries you'd like to make to your great-grandparents. Then ask yourself those questions and record your responses so that your great-grandchildren will not have to speculate on your responses. Maintain a record of your questions and replies at FamilySearch.org (click on "Memories" and then "Stories").

9. Conduct a name search. Discover the origins and significance of your last name. Alternatively, inquire of your parent how your first and middle names came to be. Keep track of what you learn.

10. locating and sharing journal entries. Share images of your ancestors' journal entries or other papers on FamilySearch.org (click on "Memories" and then "Documents"), where you may also see what others have shared about your ancestors.

11. Create a documentary on your forefathers and mothers. You can incorporate their photographs, recite passages from their journal, and perform scenes from their life.

12. Seek advice. Read ancestors' journals or speak with living relatives to identify individuals who struggled with a similar issue to yours and learn how they overcame it.

13. Organize your ancestors into a family tree. You can print a family tree at FamilySearch.org. Family trees can be made in various ways using photographs of relatives, drawing a family tree, or building a family tree—the options are nearly endless.

14. Make the most of your abilities. Consider using art, music, dance, literature, or poetry to reflect an ancestor or an ancestor's narrative.

15. Research your forefathers and mothers. Mark the locations of your ancestors' homes on a physical or digital map, along with details about what they did in each location.

16. Experiment with a new language. Acquaint yourself with genealogical jargon in the languages of your forefathers and mothers. By memorizing terms such as birth, death, marriage, and christening, you can assist others in locating their ancestors in those genealogy documents.

17. Document the origins of heirlooms. Occasionally, we lose sight of the significance of a family heirloom. Photograph the artifact and describe it on FamilySearch.org. It should be

associated with the appropriate ancestor in your Family Tree. Creating narratives will assist in preserving the significance of each thing.

18. Consult with surviving family members. Create a book or a video tribute to your living family. Inquire about their childhood experiences, key life events, favorite scriptures, and testimony.

19. Commemorate the birthday of an ancestor. Celebrate an ancestor's birthday with your family and share their memories, photos, and journal entries.

20. Make a backup of your social media posts. This is a delightful way to share your life with future generations. Additionally, you can save emails and text communications in a computer document or printouts.

21. Immerse yourself in history. Research a historical event of interest and determine whether your family was engaged or how it may have impacted their town.

22. Create a cookbook. Include family favorites or dishes that your forefathers and moms would have used in their location and period. If you have recipes from certain ancestors, save them to the profile of that ancestor on FamilySearch.org.

Conduct an immigration and military records search. Discover your ancestors' origins and destinations, the people they traveled with if they fought in a war, and the unit's history with which they fought. Numerous records can be located by conducting a name search on FamilySearch.org.

23. Educate yourself in preparation for missionary work. Once you have been called to serve a mission, you can log onto missionary.lds.org to learn more about using family history on your mission.

24. Assist others—volunteer to assist others in discovering or conducting their family history.

"Humans are the product of numerous generations of mothers and fathers. As a result, we have an innate need to connect with our forefathers and mothers. This yearning exists in all of our hearts regardless of our age. Consider the spiritual bonds made when a young woman assists her grandma in entering family information onto a computer or when a young guy discovers his great-name grandfather's on a census record. When our thoughts turn to our forefathers and mothers, something within us changes. We have a sense of belonging to something larger than ourselves. Our innate yearnings for familial ties are satisfied when we are connected to our forefathers and mothers via sacred temple rites."

The Extensive Influence of Family History

At the point when Connor M. of Texas, United States of America, consented to help with filtering tombstones for his Eagle Scout project, he had no clue the extent of his commitment. For example, a man hundreds of miles distant had been looking for information about his deceased father for two decades—since he was a small child. This man discovered the headstone image of his long-deceased father online due to Connor's work. This brought the individual face to face with several relatives he was unaware existed. As a result, he now has a loving family that he was previously unaware of. That is family history in action.

Chapter 8

How To Create An
Altar For Ancestors

You've probably seen an ancestor altar in a place of worship or during some form of cultural ceremony. One of the more prevalent displays of ancestor altars is those made for Day of the Dead in Mexico. As the name suggests, this annual observance honors those who have passed on. The entire family gathers to honor the living and the dead.

It is not necessary to commemorate and interact with the deceased every year. Instead, year-round reverence for ancestors is possible by erecting an ancestor altar in your home.

What Is an Ancestor Altar?

According to Merriam-Webster, an altar is a raised structure or location used for offering sacrifices or burning incense during worship. Consider an ancestor altar (or shrine) as a location where offerings are made, and respect is shown to the spirits of those who have gone before us.

Why Would You Establish an Ancestor Shrine?

At some point in history, cultures worldwide have practiced some ancestor veneration. While ancestral shrines are not popular in contemporary society, they have long been a feature of societies throughout. Take a few generations back, and you'll discover a long tradition of recognizing those who came before us. Therefore, why did people devote time and effort to building hallowed sites for ancestor worship? The more obvious answer is that they are part of our blood and are responsible for our existence. We would not be here if they had not traversed this Earth before us.

There is a deeper reason for reverence for ancestors than blood relationships. Our forefathers and mothers continue to be concerned about us and how we spend our lives on this physical plane.

Regardless of whether we recognize them, they are available all of the time for us. It's only natural for them to want the growth and prosperity of their descendants. Our forefathers and mothers can provide invaluable insight as we traverse our lives. They were here before us and possessed an intimate knowledge of the human condition.

Creating an ancestor altar allows us to honor the presence and guidance of our forefathers and mothers in our lives. An ancestor is anybody who has played an important part in your life. Utilize your altar to express gratitude to people who have come before you or have played a vital part in your life.

Your ancestor altar is a sacred space where you can communicate with and receive wisdom from your forefathers and mothers. You erect an altar to demonstrate to your forefathers and mothers that you cherish and welcome their communication. If you do not feel guided by your ancestors, constructing an altar space is an excellent place to start. A dedicated room for ancestors is an excellent first step toward reconnecting with them.

Who Are You Honoring?

When someone says ancestor, we immediately think of a deceased relative. While this is true, spiritual ancestors are also possible. This might be a teacher, a caregiver, or anybody else who has impacted your life. You want to ensure that you invite loving, helpful, and spiritually healthy ancestors.

What You Need for Your Altar

Preparation

An ancestor altar can be erected in any size space. To begin, you'll require a location for your altar. This could be a little desk, table, or cupboard. If the room is limited, you can also use a shelf in a cabinet or drawer. When you're in a hurry, a box works well for storing the offerings until you're ready to light the candle and make the offering. In this scenario, a wooden box or something made of a natural material would be ideal.

Following that, you'll require an altar cloth. The remainder of the altar's contents will be laid on the cloth. You'll want something made of a natural fiber that appeals to you for your altar cloth. I prefer to wear a white handwoven cloth that I discovered during a journey through the Yucatan. You can search for this altarpiece at your leisure until you discover a cloth that feels right.

Assembly

Everything that puts on top of the altar cloth serves as an invitation for your ancestor to enter the space. You'll be adding items that correspond to each of the four elements (Earth, air, fire, and water). Use a basic white candle to represent the element of fire. The color white is beneficial for attracting spirits. You should keep your candle in a place that isn't likely to catch fire.

Candles that burn for seven days are ideal for ancestral altars. They are put into a glass to assist confine the flame. Tea lights are also effective since their burn period is sufficient for rituals, and the flame can be contained within a small candle holder.

Water

Place a glass on the altar and pour a libation to represent the element of water. A libation is a beverage poured in honor of a spirit. A glass of water should be your primary libation. You may even include a drink of wine or spirits if your ancestor desired. Restock the libations as necessary.

Earth

When it comes to the earth element, you have many alternatives. Crystals, flowers, or any other object that your ancestor may have favored will suffice.

Objects may include a cigar, a deck of playing cards, or a piece of ancestral jewelry.

Additionally, you can include delicacies or desserts that your ancestor may have enjoyed. Now and again, it's wonderful to add some organic seasonal fruit to the altar. Remove the skin from fruits that you would not typically eat. For instance, peel an orange or half a pomegranate. This also contributes to the fruit's fragrance and appeal. If you are hosting or attending a celebration, keep a slice of cake for the altar. Place food items on a small platter.

Air

Incense is an excellent choice for the element of air. The smoke from the incense embodies the element of air and transports our wishes to the spirit world. You can purchase incense or manufacture your own using a combination of herbs and tree resins. Additionally, you might use a feather to symbolize the element of air.

Finishing Touches

After you've addressed the four essential components, you can add anything else you believe an ancestor might enjoy. You can also place a picture of the ancestor or family you honor on the altar. Ancestors should be in good health before they may be included in your family tree. Were you close to your ancestors, whether your father or mother? Was their demise distressing in any way? Before adding images of ancestors to the altar, make sure to mend any disruptions.

You allow these spirits into your area, and you want to ensure they bring only positive energy.

Additionally, ensure that none of the photographs on the altar depicts somebody who is still alive. Additionally, you may like to include something personal that you have created, such as a piece of artwork.

Checklist for Ancestor Altars

- Table or shelf

- Altar robe

- Candle

- Incense

- Water glass

- Photographs and memorials personnel

Keeping the Ancestor Altar or Shrine in Good Condition

Maintain a nice and orderly altar—dust and re-hydrate the water regularly. If you add flowers, dispose of the old ones in the natural environment. Fresh food plates should be removed and discarded within 24 hours. You do not want anything rotten or moldy on your altar, even more so if you are honoring an exceptionally clean ancestor! Once fully mature, fruits that have not been peeled can be removed.

Your ancestor altar is a place where you can commune with your guides regularly. Establishing an altar is the first significant step toward cultivating a relationship that has the potential to last a lifetime.

As you become acquainted with your forefathers and mothers, you will recognize the various ways they manifest themselves in daily life. Spend time at your altar conversing with your forefathers and mothers. You can converse with them like you would with a buddy.

Maintain communication with them now that you've created this hallowed space in their honor.

Create an Ancestor Shrine - Create an Ancestor Altar

In many Pagan traditions, particularly around Samhain, the ancestors are venerated. After all, this Sabbat is the night when the curtain between our world and the spirit world is most difficult. By erecting an ancestor shrine or altar, you can pay tribute to the members of your bloodline–your relatives and clan members who have shaped who you are. Alternatively, this altar or shrine can be used for rituals and meditation throughout the year.

Paying Tribute to Those Who Came Before Us

A full table dedicated to this shrine is fantastic, but if you're short on space, you may make it in the corner of your dresser, a shelf, or even above your fireplace. If you put your ancestors and moms in a spot where they can be left undisturbed, you can meditate and honor them without constantly shifting things about. Include a deceased pet or companion if you choose. It is not necessary for someone to be blood-related to be a member of our spiritual ancestry.

Make the Space Special

To begin, thoroughly clean the space. After all, would you encourage Aunt Gertrude to sit in a filthy chair? Next, dust the tabletop or shelf and remove any non-shrine-related things. You may dedicate the place as sacred if you like by stating something along the lines of:

In honor of those whose blood runs through my veins, I use this space: my forefathers and mothers, my guides and protectors, and those whose spirits shaped me. Smudge the area with sage, sweetgrass,

Asperger, and holy water. You may decide to consecrate the place with all four elements if your tradition requires it.

Finally, incorporate an altar cloth to assist in welcoming the ancestors. A red cloth is always used in many Eastern religions. A fringe on the altar cloth is said to assist in connecting your Spirit to those of your ancestors in some Celtic-based religions. If you have time before Samhain, you may like to create an ancestor altar cloth containing information about your genealogy.

Welcome Your Clan and Kin

There are numerous types of ancestors, and the ones you add are entirely up to you. First, our blood ancestors are the individuals directly descended from us: parents, grandparents, etc. Additionally, some archetypical forebears reflect the origins of our clan and family. Additionally, some people choose to commemorate the Land's ancestors–the spirits of the area you are now–to express gratitude. Finally, our spiritual ancestors are those we are not related to by blood or marriage but whom we yet regard as family.

Begin by selecting photographs of your forefathers and mothers. Choose images that have importance for you–and it's acceptable if the images include live people and the deceased. Then, arrange the photographs on your altar so that you can view them all at once.

If you do not have a photograph of an ancestor, you might substitute an item from their possession. For example, if you're honoring someone who lived before the mid-1800s, there is no photograph of them. Rather than that, use an object that was maybe the person's–jewelry, a dish from your family heirloom set, a family Bible, etc.

Additionally, you can incorporate ancestral symbols. For example, if your family originates in Scotland, you can represent your clan with a kilt button or a length of plaid. If you hail from a family of artisans, wear an item made or created to represent your ancestors' artisanship.

Finally, you can embellish the shrine with a genealogy sheet or family tree. If you have the ashes of a departed loved one, include those.

Once you've gathered everything representing your ancestors in your shrine, try adding a few other items. For example, certain individuals choose to include votive candles, which they can light while meditating. You may decide to include a cauldron or cup to represent the Earth Mother's womb. Additionally, you can include a spiritual symbol, such as a pentagram, an ankh, or another expression of your beliefs.

Some people also place food offerings on their altars so that their forefathers and mothers might share a meal with the family. Utilize the altar when doing a Samhain ancestor meditation or an ancestor-honoring ritual.

How to Build an Ancestor Altar
to Honor Your Forgotten Ancestors

Setting up an ancestor altar is critical if you're just beginning to create a relationship with your ancestors. It provides a regular venue for communication. It acts as a reminder that your forefathers and mothers are still alive. Here is a step-by-step guide to erecting an ancestral altar. Additionally, how to maintain it.

How to Build an Ancestor Altar: A Step-by-Step Guide

Do not be concerned with how altars seem online. Do not even consider how altars appear in your head. Concentrate on the energy you placed into your ancestor altar when you originally set it up. Yours will be unlike any other...because it will be uniquely yours. And your forefathers and mothers will be overjoyed to have an actual location to visit.

1. Decide on a Surface

To begin, choose a location for your altar. I strongly advise against placing it in your bedroom. However, perhaps in your living room, dining area, or kitchen. Your forefathers and mothers do not wish to see what you do in your spare time. Following that, select a table, buffet, shelf, or counter that will be utilized purely to commemorate your forefathers and mothers. This means that nothing else will be affixed to it. There are no phones, remote controls, computers, televisions, or other appliances. An excellent option is a wall shelf, an empty bookshelf, or a tiny accent table.

2. Assemble Your Ancestor Altar's Tools and Supplies

Following that, pick what you want to include on your ancestral altar. A few basic suggestions: a photograph(s) of your ancestors, heirlooms, offering cup and bowl, incense and an incense burner, candles, candleholders, and seasonal decorations (optional). Suppose you do not have photographs of your forefathers and mothers, objects that represent them and connect you to their energy function just as well. Heirlooms are advantageous in this regard. What if you, too, lack heirlooms? A map of their homeland, photographs of historical markers, and similar items can be used instead of personal photographs.

3. Cleansing

After selecting a surface and assembling your equipment, it's time to cleanse. There are several ways to cleanse your altar, including using smoke, aspiring, or washing the surface and equipment with a towel. If you prefer to clean them, use a solution of lemon juice and water. While cleansing, picture a white light shining down from above, lighting the altar's surface and each item.

4. Set-Up

Following that, it's time to erect your ancestor altar. The configuration is completely up to you. Certain faiths and religions, such as Wicca, may have a prescribed design; however, if you're lonely and doing this on your own, you can build it up as you like! I prefer to start with my ancestors, make their photographs the focal point, and build around them. Spring and summer bring flowers, summer brings fruits and vegetables, fall brings pumpkins, and winter brings Christmas decorations. These are some of the things I like to incorporate into my design. Not to be forgotten - welcome your forefathers and mothers to our space!

5. Provide Offerings

When you set up your ancestral altar, make offerings and invite your forefathers and mothers to this sacred location. A fresh cup of water, flowers, incense, a candle flame, beverages such as wine and coffee, fruit, and food, in general, are all acceptable offerings. Over time, your forefathers and mothers will communicate which offers they prefer and which ones they reject. Believe me, and you will soon hear their voices.

How to Keep Your Ancestor Altar in Good Condition

You've built up your ancestor altar, but what now? First, utilize your altar as a concrete, tangible space in which you can communicate with your ancestors. It makes no difference whether you speak out or in your mind. Additionally, make regular offerings. Certain individuals make daily offerings. I make weekly offerings. At the same time, some may donate only once every two weeks. Additional offerings to ancestors include homemade objects, poetry, singing, artwork, and pretty much anything else you feel moved to offer.

Allow your altar to be a source of inspiration. When you are sad, unwell, or in need, stand at your ancestral shrine and invoke the help of your forefathers and mothers. Three times knock and yell their names out (if you know the names). Then, light a candle in their honor and inform them that it is in their honor.

Never forget to sanitize your ancestor's altar regularly. I love to keep mine clean and cleansed once a month — generally on the New

Moon. I dust the altar and supplies and then cleanse with smoke or blessed water/spray. After reconnecting, I welcome my ancestors' presence to return to the space.

Chapter 9

Offerings For An Ancestor Altar
(Friendly For Beginners And Advanced!)

Creating an ancestor altar with whom to work regularly is a powerful ritual that energizes spirit work. It's an excellent approach to connect with both your ancestors and yourself. Strengthening your connection to your ancestral army will assist you in being grounded and properly guided.

GETTING STARTED:

I detailed how to set up a simple ancestral altar in this part, but all you need to get started is a small table, preferably covered in white table linen. You may cleanse the table, cloth, and space energetically using your favorite medium if you like. Maintain this table outside of your bedroom or other sleeping areas.

This will be the altar or shrine dedicated to your ancestors. You can meditate and perform spirit work here, leave offerings, or revere your forefathers and mothers.

A few of these fundamental offerings to have on an ancestor altar include the following:

- Photographs of deceased family members and friends. Typically, I see framed photographs on ancestral shrines, but I have also placed obituaries on my altar.

- Candlelight. When using candles, you must either sit with the light (in a meditative manner, if desired) or be preset while the candle is lighted.

- Cold, fresh water in transparent glass. You'll need to replace this water on a regular/weekly basis.

Are you interested in learning more about the uses of your ancestral altar? I'd love to write a post for you if you're interested. If so, please inform me in the comments section!

INTERMEDIATE:

For more complex services, others may require more attention or maintenance regularly. Several of these items may prompt you to sit actively with your ancestor altar or to tend to the artifacts daily to prevent them from spoiling.

- Incense/Cigar smoke

- Flowers

- Black Coffee

- Fresh Fruit

- A portion of your daily meals

- Incense/Cigar smoke

OTHER IDEAS FOR ANCESTOR WORK:

If you are so inclined, consult with and speak with your forefathers and mothers about any tiny special offerings that could be included. Suppose you're looking for further ideas for particular goods to gift your ancestors at their ancestral shrine. In that case, you can include additional personal objects you may have or even prepare you may want to incorporate additional personal family artifacts to your ancestral shrine:

- One-of-a-kind meal/foods. Even if you are not a meat-eater, your forefathers and mothers may appreciate an occasional offering of backfat or turkey necks (for example). Alternatively, you might make a modest bit of another traditional meal popular with your ancestors that you may not enjoy for your ancestor table.

- If your ancestor table requires it, ancestral crops/agriculture such as cotton and sugarcane are excellent adds.

- Cigarettes, Tobacco Chewing Devices, Cigars, and Other Tobacco Products. Look for those your deceased family members used if you are familiar with brands.

- Jewelry and priceless family heirlooms

- The Bible, prayer books, and other sacred literature

- While liquor is frequently offered to ancestors, please keep in mind that with so many families having a history of alcoholism, it may not be something you want to include on your table. Utilize your best judgment.

Whether you merely provide cool water or elaborate meals to your ancestors, tending an ancestor table daily can help establish relationships with guides.

Historically, how does your culture honor those who have come before us? Are there any motifs or objects that symbolize your family? Meditate with your ancestral table, and if any suggestions for offerings that might be appropriate for your shrine occur to you, jot them down and fulfill them as soon as possible.

It is critical to maintaining a connection with yourself and your guides while performing this activity. Certain questions you can answer for yourself using logic, personal experience, intuition, and your magnificent mind. How are you feeling? Which of the accompanying sounds good to you? While performing this task, ask yourself these critical questions, as it is individualized for you, your requirements, and your resources. If you cannot afford a table, your altar may have to remain on the ground for a time. If you lack space for an altar, you may need to discover alternative ways to connect with and revere your ancestors. Please remember that the rules are changeable because we are all unique.

Altar items: Keep in mind that everything you set on the altar should not be worn or used in the future. Therefore, if you place food on the altar, you must remove it the following day. Consume no food or leave it on the altar. If you place jewelry on the altar, you should refrain from wearing it unless it is necessary for some form of ritual. I would not recommend placing a piece of jewelry on the altar if you wish to continue wearing it regularly. When I place food on the altar, I use a special chipped plate that I do not use for anything else. I recommend using a chipped plate for a tiny food offering and a chipped mug for coffee. For water, obtain a transparent glass that will remain on the altar.

You may use any food. Because I set the table daily, I set the table with food that I generally eat and items they may consume, such as white bread and bacon. Because I am not connected to you, I cannot tell you what your great-grandmother would want on that table. This is the point at which you must exercise your imagination and intellect.

You are not required to set out an entire dinner for them unless you like to. For example, a small slice of bread with meat, a scoop of vegetables, or a piece of fruit are all acceptable.

Food disposal: Food should be discarded the next day. Leave no stale food on an altar. Allow no food to spoil on the altar. You can either toss away the food or compost it. Dispose of it before going to bed or the next morning.

Food and beverages should be discarded regularly. It's important to refill your water glass frequently. For some, this may occur daily or weekly. Twice a month, or monthly, is a decent interval for me. You do not require a ritual to remove the food, my friends. Discard it. If you feel this activity requires a ritual, connect with yourself and YOUR ancestors and construct one. Make the best of what you have. Utilize your knowledge, your experiences, and your sources of information.

Make an altar: Ideally, your altar should be on a table, but it can also be on the floor. That has been done numerous times previously, and while it is not the way I was taught, it makes logic. These are our ancestors; why would they not be on the ground? Create a makeshift table using another elevated surface if you want them elevated but lack the space or budget for a table.

You do not want to place an altar in your bedroom, as they require a distinct area. If your ancestors are night owls, they may keep you awake. They require their own space to ensure that you can enjoy some uninterrupted calm. This is done to create a space for your ancestral line to communicate close by, but not necessarily on top of you. If that made no sense, the message is probably not for you. My apologies for not providing additional clarification. Certain concepts cannot be over-explained to the inexperienced.

Chapter 10

How Do I Make Contact
With My Ancestors?

This is particularly beneficial during sadness and loss, but ancestors are also necessary on the dharmic path. Spirit and the ancestors can be of great help to anyone in need of guidance in their lives, but most people are unaware of this. We frequently forget that our forefathers and mothers are here to assist and guide us.

When a loved one passes into Spirit, they become available to assist us in ways that they could not do while in physical form.

However, we frequently associate our human experiences with our ancestors. After someone has passed on to the spirit world, we may find it difficult to connect with them because of resentments, hurdles, and other challenging parts of the interpersonal dynamic. Indeed, this is a critical aspect of the grief journey—identifying and honoring human emotions while also leaving room for something new to enter. By releasing unprocessed emotions, a new prospective relationship with Spirit can arise.

Resisting and suppressing these unprocessed feelings that are an inescapable aspect of the relationship will prevent you from connecting with your ancestors.

This is why so many people feel no connection to their forefathers or mothers. Resisting or avoiding sadness, difficult emotions, unpleasant memories, wounds, and lineage traumas can result in severing and avoiding the ancestral connection. This is a compelling reason to pay attention to your sadness diligently and use it as a source of healing.

We acknowledge our humanity and our emotional bodies at the same time when we do this. To make room for something new to come, it's important to let go of things that no longer serve you, such as feelings and emotions. There is practically no room for anything else to enter if the body is clogged with unprocessed grief and emotions.

Allowing grief to flow allows for the arrival of new life and increased resiliency. Eliminating sadness from the bodies creates space for the Spirit to enter while also facilitating the possibility of developing a relationship with the ancestors. When we lose touch with our forefathers and mothers, we also lose the thread of dharma, legacy, and the potent resources that weave the family line together.

Remember that your human bond with your forefathers and mothers is not the entire narrative.

We must pay attention to the human aspects while still making room for Spirit. Once a loved one has merged with Spirit, they can serve as an ally and support in ways not conceivable while in human form. After they leave the limits of the body container, there is an opportunity to develop a new relationship with them. By connecting with our ancestors, we can establish a fresh relationship with people in Spirit, even if we had a difficult relationship with them when they were human or had no connection with them.

Your willingness to be candid about your sentiments, grief, emotions, and personal mythology opens the door to clearing, healing, and releasing your lineage's buried wounds, trauma, and challenges.

Because the ancestors are not alive, they cannot change, transform, or evolve—at least not without your assistance. You are the lynchpin that holds them together. You are the living being capable of assisting the lineage in changing, transforming, and growing. Your healing journey and dharmic path are critical components of your ancestors' and family line's change. If you choose not to undertake your dharmic task, you will profoundly affect the ancestors' lineage and growth if you oppose your life purpose and the necessary healing.

Dharma is the most effective approach to pay tribute to the ancestors.

Nothing is more important than dharma from a Vedic standpoint. Indeed, this is the sole reason you took on a human form. Nonetheless, most people who inhabit a human body never fully connect with their life path or purpose over their lifetime. Regrettably, hurdles, fears, delusions, and impediments to the path prevent most individuals from truly accepting their dharma.

Regrettably, this opposition to dharma has a detrimental effect on the ancestors. Contrary to dharma, adharma produces ignorance and suffering. When dharma is lost, the family lineage's healing, growth, and vitality deteriorate. Generations of repressed emotions, sadness, and trauma have culminated in the global loss of dharma.

Nowadays, it is extremely difficult to live by one's dharma.

Dharma, in my opinion, demands reciprocity. You are simultaneously healing yourself, your lineage, and others by awakening and sharing your abilities, wisdom, and mission with the world. This demands considerable diligence and introspection. It is not a road that everyone picks or even understands exists. When adharma takes hold, the connection to the ancestors is also weakened. The healing path is required to awaken one's gifts, purpose, and wisdom inherited from one's ancestors.

Bear in mind that this is also the time of the Kali Yuga, according to the Vedic Calendar. This is a moment of immense degeneration and disorder. Dharma is virtually nonexistent. Finding one's way is a tremendous accomplishment. However, it is stated that if and when you can align with your dharma, attaining full awakening and enlightenment would be easier. Dharma and awakening are inextricably linked.

It is essential to connect with one's ancestors for healing and transformation to occur.

A connection to one's ancestors is also critical for improving one's dharmic path. The ancestors are present, waiting for you to reach out to them for assistance, resources, and advice. They are genuinely interested in developing a relationship with you. Ancestors can manifest in a variety of ways through a range of experiences. Occasionally, you will sense their presence; they will manifest themselves through visuals at other times. For example, my mum and father frequently communicate with me through owl and hawk medication. You will begin to understand their lessons as you accept them into your life. Bear in mind that Nature may also impart inherited wisdom to you. The ancestors may communicate with us through our physical, mental, emotional, or spiritual bodies. Pay close attention.

There are healthy and unhealthy forebears. Guidance and assisting spirits. Nature spirits and animal guides. The collective ancestry of all forebears, as well as your lineage. There are helpful and malicious ancestors. We want to be clear about the ancestors we wish to communicate with. Additionally, it is critical to communicate what is unacceptable to you.

I recall one of my teachers delivering a poignant lesson about the need to set boundaries and intentions with our forefathers and mothers. Sobonfu Some, a Dagara elder, stated that she frequently yelled and cursed at her ancestors and then starved them for days if she was furious with them. Never lose sight of the fact that you are in control of the connection! Inform them of your emotions: wrath, rage, sadness, grief, joy, or thankfulness. They regard your emotions as nourishment. They consume it, compost it, and convert it to pure energy. It is your responsibility to recognize and release it. Maintain a flowing, flowing, and dancing emotional body, similar to a river.

Developing a relationship with one's ancestors is similar to developing any other relationship.

It necessitates diligence, constancy, presence, and a readiness to learn. To re-establish a link with your ancestors, you must be willing to feed them daily. I recommend feeding them every day and establishing routines to facilitate this process.

Here are six methods to nourish your ancestors and deepen your relationship with them:

1) Construct an altar or shrine to the ancestors.

If feasible, position this altar towards the east (so you are facing east when you look at it). The east is the direction of daybreak, and the objective is to bring light to oneself and one's ancestors. Collect artifacts that remind your forefathers and mothers to place statues, photographs, souvenirs, and natural offerings on the shrine. Arrange something alive on the altar, such as a plant. A bowl of spring water (ideally) and sea salt can aid in the clearing of emotional blocks. Regularly replenish this water and never allow it to stagnate. Consistently bring offerings to your altar and express gratitude to the ancestors' advice. Light a candle, burn palo santo, and invoke your goal to maintain a regular connection with your ancestors. Keep this altar clean at all times. Make this altar outside of your bedroom, bathroom, or kitchen. Locate or develop a communal living place outdoors.

2) Bring food offerings.

Cooking and sharing a piece of your meals with your ancestors is one of the most important ways I connect with my ancestors. This potent symbolizes gratitude, recognizing and physically connecting with your forefathers and mothers via the quality of life energy. Each day as you prepare your meals, place a small portion of your food in a bowl and place it on your altar. Inform your forefathers and mothers of why you are feeding them—what you are grateful for and what needs you have. Allow no more than 24 hours for this dish to sit. Once the ancestors have been adequately fed, compost the food, allow it to return to Nature, or feed it to a companion animal. You can also consume the food to imbibe the Spirit of the ancestors.

3) Grief Rituals.

Attending to your grief is a critical component of developing a relationship with your ancestors. Your emotions are a source of nourishment for them. They take your anguish and consume it like nourishment. They are eager for your anguish, even crave it. Your ability to connect with your sorrow, hardships, suffering, and unresolved emotions can be tremendously aided by your forefathers and mothers. They are genuinely committed to assisting you during this process. In addition, grieving regularly is vital for overall body health and balance. Unprocessed emotions accumulate in the body and must be cleaned regularly to make room for life, joy, and plenty. Developing a practice of grieving allows you to nourish the ancestors and release and expel stagnant energy in your body. This is perfect if you can participate in formal grief rituals numerous times. Consider it a seasonal grief cleansing!

4) Incorporate rituals into your daily life.

Rituals function similarly to spiritual containers. They provide a sacred framework to connect with the unseen, the hidden, and the realms beyond the commonplace. This cloak of illusion serves as a reminder that there is more to life than what we see on the surface of things. Rituals can be straightforward or opulent. I'm offering basic, persistent routines that will assist you in connecting with Spirit regularly. Creating regular touchstones to aid in connection is an important component of developing a relationship with your ancestors. It's a simple matter of making it a habit to take a few moments to check in, listen, and notice. To bring presence to Spirit and your complete body physical, mental, emotional, and spiritual. Take a moment to check, notice, and breathe. What is on its way? Where do you experience a sense of connection? Disconnected? Do you have a sense of connection to Spirit? Or do you have a sense of disconnection? What messages are being delivered?

5) Spend time in Nature.

Bear in mind that Spirit is Nature and Nature is Spirit. They are synonymous. When we spend enough time in Nature, we become more adept at merging with Her wisdom. We align with the innate oneness that exists inside and around us all. Nature may inspire awe and serve as a reminder of how genuinely strong Spirit is. Daily, if feasible, spend time in Nature. It's a simple matter of making it a habit to take a few moments to check in, listen, and notice. The ancestors are in every rock, tree, sky, earth, and animal. Take note of the things Spirit may wish to convey to you regarding your truth, purpose, and ancestral wisdom. Inquire about messages and pay close attention to the responses.

6) Reignite your dharma.

Your life path and purpose are the ultimate means to provide for your forefathers and mothers. You can't give your ancestors a better present than this. By aligning with your truth and inner wisdom, awakening and sharing your abilities with the world, you are blessing your lineage. Both you and your forefathers and mothers are blessed by the gifts and fullness of this voyage. Dharma necessitates that you lean into your difficulties, sadness, pain, hardships, and suffering. It means that you are willing to develop, heal, and grow due to confronting your darkness honestly and courageously. Dharma is not a passive path, nor is it for the faint-hearted. The rewards, however, extend beyond this lifetime and this terrestrial sphere. Living your mission, sharing your abilities with the world, and assisting others in their healing and awakening is the most powerful offering you can make to your lineage!

Bear in mind that your forefathers are never far away. They are anxiously awaiting your acknowledgment and acceptance into your life. Allow yourself to be receptive to their message in all its manifestations. Be observant and present in the ways they manifest. Even if no messages are received, they continue to appear. At some point, the space you are creating for them to enter will pay off. Above all, attend to your sadness and embrace your journey of recovery. Alignment with one's dharma is the primary reason for existence in the human body. Solicit guidance and help from your ancestors during this process.

How to Communicate With Your Ancestors

The yearning to interact with our forefathers and mothers is ingrained in the human experience. We intuitively perceive their presence in our wisdom bodies, which begs the question: are we capable of communicating with them?

The ancestor spirits can communicate, lead, defend, and heal the living through daily prayer, mediation, the creation of art, music, food, and ceremony. Ancestral communication has been an old practice in every wisdom system. Your power to communicate with your forefathers and mothers is perpetual.

The period from the 31st of October to the 2nd of November, in particular, represents a pivotal point in human evolution. It is the transitional season between fall and winter, the season of death and dying. As a result, now is an excellent moment to interact with one's ancestors. This essay will walk you through the steps of making a beautiful ceremonial journey that will allow you to connect with your ancestors on a deeper level.

The Traditions of Ancestral Communication

Mayan, Celtic, Aborigine, Indigenous American, Ancient Greece, Ancient Eurasia, and African Tribal and Vedic/Yoga traditions have a long history of ancestor-to-ancestor communication. Some major religions, such as Catholicism, observe All Saints Day and All Souls Day honor the deceased by reciting prayers and lighting candles and incense. Mexico commemorates the Day of the Dead (Dia De Los Muertos). Additionally, in the Celtic tradition, Samhain commemorates the moment of transition between the two worlds.

We are all familiar with Halloween or All Hallows Eve in our culture. As a result, the spiritual knowledge and soul of the ritual days, which were meant to memorialize and communicate with the ancestor spirits, have been mostly lost.

When I was a kid, my father passed away. By connecting with my father and ancestors, I have been able to widen my heart and experience more love for myself. In addition, I've been able to heal profound hurts and karmic patterns that extend beyond my father and my deceased grandparents and living relatives through this process. Ancestral work can modify the karmas of previous generations and work to cure the current and future generations.

Halloween and The Day of the Dead

Historically, these two occasions have been regarded as ceremonial days and nights dedicated to honoring and communicating with one's ancestors. This is an opportunity to make family altars, conduct ancestral rites, and arrange flowers, incense, crystals, art, and food offerings. Halloween, often known as All Hallows Eve, literally translates as Holy Night or All Saints' Night. Ancestors, saints, and those who have crossed over to the other side can all be remembered and connected. The Day of the Dead retains the spiritual core of ceremonial honor and communication in Mexico's interior.

I was in southern Mexico last year, in the city of Merida, studying the Mayan tradition. Walking around in the main square two days before Day of the Dead, I decided to take a break from my preparations and enjoy the night air. I came across a local celebration. Throughout the central plaza, dozens of families from surrounding towns enthusiastically created altars, cooked and shared food, lit candles, erected their deceased images, and played music. Their prayers and offerings lifted my Spirit to their ancestors, and I could feel the presence of the divine filling the space around me.

Elements of these lovely rites and altar practices can be seen in our modern Halloween through the use of candles in jack-o-lanterns, candy offerings, and celebrations. During this time of year, when the curtain between the two worlds is open, you can actively reconnect with these old customs.

Who is an Ancestor?

Mitakuye Oyasin translates as "All are my kin" in Lakota. This includes the tree, water, sky, soil, animals, brothers, sisters, and those who have taken their spiritual walk. A holy hoop, a medicine wheel, and a life mandala are all included. Everything is interconnected. Everything is alive and has the essence of Love. All are spiritual and bodily children of the Great Mother and Father.

An ancestor is someone who assumed a physical form and went through the loves, tragedies, joys, and hardships of human existence. Your parents, aunts, uncles, grandparents, and great grandparents are there. Anyone who has participated in a spirit walk. Any member of your soul tribe.

The ancestors are those who have a firsthand understanding of what it's like to take on the human form and share your spiritual and physical DNA. They have a high capacity for empathy, compassion, and sensitivity to the experience of being on a personal earth trip. They can impart beneficial teachings, guidance, protection, healing, and forgiveness from the spirit plane. Ancestors, as spiritual beings, may likewise need healing and evolution, and they are still seen as an integral part of life's holy hoop.

There are Territorial Ancestors (also known as Land Ancestors) and Spiritual Ancestors. Territorial or Land Ancestors are creatures who take on the form of a piece of Land and become spiritual guardians and stewards of the Land. If you live/work on ancestral grounds, your family ancestors may also be your Territorial Ancestors. Your Spiritual Ancestors are a lineage of spirit beings with whom your soul has chosen to work frequently. This might be Archangel Michael, Buddha, Quan Yin (also known as Guanyin), White Buffalo Calf Woman, Pleiadian Star Beings, or Egyptian wisdom spirits—the possibilities are endless. Infinite possibilities exist, and a family member may fit into "categories."

We will focus on your soul tribal ancestors during our ritual of communicating with your ancestors. It is OK to invite members of your other ancestral lines to attend and lend assistance.

Why Is It Necessary to Communicate with Your Ancestors?

When my father, Robert Schenkelberg, died suddenly in 2003 of a blood clot in his lungs, I was far from resolving several issues with him. Instead, there was a mix of intense Love, anguish, uncertainty, wrath, despair, and numerous unsolved questions regarding certain childhood situations. At the time, I was uninterested in spiritual connections and even avoided them.

Ten years passed, and I gradually lost touch with my own heart. Finally, I found myself at a mountain ashram pursuing inner peace, reading a book about a spiritual teacher who predicted his demise. Inviting all of his students to join him, the teacher explained that they are not physically gone when someone dies but remain present in Love. They have ascended to the ethereal realms and remain with us.

He stated that we could choose to honor and cherish them. This statement reawakened my soul and opened the door to a profound spiritual heart transformation. In October 2013, at the juncture of fall and winter, my father communicated with me in a dream. Over three years, it has evolved through prayer, meditation, ceremony, daily discourse, and a willingness to surrender to greater development. However, the most significant way to healing for me, his Spirit, my grandparents, and even my living family - my mother, brother, sister, cousins, aunts, and uncles - has been this connection with my father. By opening your heart and developing the ability to interact with your ancestors, you can experience profound, transformative healing on all levels.

When I communicate with my father and ancestors, I experience many moments of delight and contentment. They laugh beside me, send me messages in the wind, fly in on the wings of a hawk, console me with their Love, and provide loving advice for my soul's destiny in this life. Of course, this involves personal work – dissolving ingrained programming, emotions, grudges, and stories – and will continue to do so. But, for me, the most potent and satisfying gift of my spiritual journey has been ancestor contact and healing.

Why Should You Perform Ceremonies to Communicate with Your Ancestors?

There are numerous methods for communicating with your forefathers and mothers, and it may gradually become a daily habit and dialogue for you. Simply inviting them into your heart and spending some peaceful time with them can be ideal. Ceremonies, on the other hand, can serve to intensify communication.

Spirit is energy that communicates with the earthy plane via high vibration frequencies. Ceremonies are charged with strong vibration. The distinction between an offering ritual and personal prayer is analogous to playing the guitar acoustically and amplified. Both are lovely and suitable for various purposes, but one has greater resonance and reach. Just like it is easier for us to hear an amplified guitar, the higher vibration of ceremony makes it easier for the Spirit to connect with us.

We have conducted ceremonies numerous times on our own, in groups, at our yoga studio, on retreats, and with individuals of diverse faiths and beliefs. We have discovered that most people, even in their first experience, have an inbuilt memory and attachment to ritual.

What exactly is a ceremony?

Numerous ancient wisdom traditions on our planet share the gift of the ceremony, and ceremonies can be performed in various ways— individually or in groups. While the ceremony's intricacies may vary, three universal components apply anywhere, anytime:

1. Intention: In the yoga tradition, this is referred to as Sankalpa, which translates as "heart promise." Declare your objective. It can take the form of a positive affirmation, a request for an answer to a question, or a prayer for healing.

2. Concentration: Maintain a state of alertness. Alternatively, as Ram Dass puts it, "Be Here Now." Establish a firm foundation in your heart and calm your mind. Wherever your attention goes, energy flows.

3. Meaningful: Ensure that your actions are meaningful to you. When you are participating in a group ceremony, there may be things that

do not resonate with you at the time. That is acceptable. Maintain your focus on your inner intention, the gift you are making from your heart. As you create your unique wedding ceremony, make sure it is meaningful.

How to Construct an Ancestral Ritual

After completing the fundamental three, you are ready to build your Ancestral Ceremony and reopen the connection lines. The following is a list of possible ingredients for your ancestral – or any – ceremony:

Establish Sacred Space

Locate a suitable location for your ceremony: being outside in Nature or a calm space inside is strongly recommended. Create an altar for your forefathers and mothers. This may involve the following:

- Clearing the energy and opening the gateway using incense, copal, sage, or palo santo

- Candles, flowers, a basin of water, crystals, shells, feathers, tobacco, corn, or grains are examples of natural elements.

- photographs, heirlooms, and mementos of the ancestors, such as a ring, a pocketknife, a book, or even a recipe book

- Spiritual relics, such as your favorite deity, prayer flags, or anything else that represents Spirit to you

- Rattles, drums, bells, gongs, or singing bowls to open up the portal through sound

Permission Requests and Invitations

Permission, guidance, and protection from Spirit are required to perform your ritual. Invite your Spirit Guides and Angels to assist you, and invite any ancestors you wish to be present at the event by name.

Call in the Directions

Solicit the presence of the spirits of the Four Directions, Mother Earth, and Father Sky during the ceremony.

Make Offerings

Offer an ancestor(s) a handwritten letter that can be burned and carried to Spirit via smoke. Alternatively, make a public statement to the deceased. Following your speech, make an offering of the altar objects you choose.

Take a Moment

Sit quietly and connect with Spirit and your ancestors' energy. Concentrate on your original intent. Pay close attention to any messages in your heart, head, and body. You may receive an instantaneous knowing, an image, a sensation, inner light, Love, or even spoken communication. Alternatively, it could simply be a tranquil repose. Spirit responds in divine order. Additional information may be revealed through dreams, Nature, and future interactions.

Music and Mantra

You may select a song, a mantra, or a chant that resonates with you. It can be complemented by your voice or instruments such as drums and rattles to evoke Mother Earth's primordial heartbeat.

Guided Journey (Optional)

Consider a guided excursion frequently conducted by a shaman or someone skilled in guided meditation.

Conclude the Ceremonies

Bring the Four Directions, Mother Earth and Father Sky, to a close. Express gratitude to your Spirit Guides and Angels for their support and send your forefathers and mothers the last blessing.

Celebration and Reflection

Share some food, water, music, and conversation with loved ones, and keep a notebook to document your feelings and experiences.

Be receptive to whatever occurs. Spirit can arrive in a whisper or a cosmic thump to the head. And it can arrive immediately or when you least expect it. What is critical is your intention, focus, and purpose. The seeds you have sown will thrive if nurtured with a sincere heart. Have faith in the process. May your forefathers and mothers be with you.

Chapter 11

Tutorial On Ancestor Prayer:
Invoking The Assistance Of Ancestors

My ancestors are a critical element of my spiritual practice. Worship of ancestors is widespread worldwide but is notably prevalent in China, Vietnam, sections of Africa, Mexico, and certain indigenous American groups. Some pagans are beginning to see the value of ancestor veneration - it helps you connect with your ancestors and provides opportunities for spiritual growth and blessings. Frequently, people are perplexed as to where, to begin with, ancestor worship. I recommend starting with ancestor prayer, which appeals to ancestors for healing, protection, and comfort.

Additionally, guess what? Praying to your forefathers and mothers is not as tough as you may believe. They are a part of you, which makes them highly accessible. Therefore, it is irrelevant whether you believe your ancestors are floating about in space or have reincarnated. They are completely accessible because of that unbreakable relationship — your lineage.

Ancestor Prayer: A Few Ways to Pray

Ancestor prayer can be performed in various ways, depending on your comfort level. First, you can pray formally to the ancestors in the same way you would any other god or goddess. If you begin your prayers with "Dear God," begin your ancestor prayer with "Dear Ancestors." Alternatively, you may begin with "Blessed Ancestors" or "Beloved Ancestors." Then resume your prayer. Whether you're seeking assistance in a particular area or expressing gratitude for their presence in your life, any manner is acceptable! Typically, I begin my ancestor's prayer with a word of appreciation and then make requests for things I require. Additionally, I will conclude my ancestral prayer with a phrase such as "so be it," "so mote it be," or "and it comes to pass."

Some people are uncomfortable praying in such a formal manner to their ancestors. Perhaps it evokes memories of a religion they abandoned long ago. This is OK as well! Additionally, ancestral prayer can take the form of a casual dialogue with a friend or family member. Bear in mind that your forefathers and mothers are your families! Therefore, address them like a mother, father, aunt, uncle, or cousin. You are not required to make a formal opening speech or conclude with "amen" or "thus be it," etc. Politely, conclude your ancestral prayer by saying "good night" or "that's all for now!"

What if I had been adopted or was separated from my family?

You are not required to know your ancestors' names. Once again, your forefathers and mothers are a bodily part of you. They exist because of you. Praying to the ancestors is as straightforward as referring to them as "ancestors." Therefore, even if you were adopted and have no knowledge of your forefathers or mothers, you can still pray to them.

They remain present to assist and protect you. Are you estranged from family members? The same holds.

Rhyming Prayers

I used to say that rhyming is irrelevant in prayers and chants. However, in real honesty, rhyming assists us in concentrating our intentions and raising heavenly energy. While rhyming prayers do not have to be recited constantly, they are beneficial when focused on a specific objective. And they are easily repeatable. If you need an ancestral healing prayer, you may wish to write one for yourself. Even if you are the "worst writer," you will eventually create a poetic ancestor prayer that you may memorize and use! When extra effort is made to communicate with the ancestors, they appreciate it. It's similar to writing a poem for a family member — wouldn't you feel honored if someone wrote you a poem? It's all about communication and appreciation!

Ancestor Prayer for Protection

Ancestors within me

Wild and free

Guide and protect me

For eternity

Ancestral Healing Prayer

Blessed Ancestors hear me this night

Grant me your love and healing light

Ancestral Abundance Prayer

Money flow freely to me and my family

Money flow freely

For the highest good of all

Ancestors make it be.

Calling on Ancestors for Help

It's as straightforward as what I stated previously. Invoking the assistance of ancestors does not have to be complicated or extravagant. It's good to remember how much your forefathers and mothers appreciated gifts. Create a tiny ancestor altar in their honor or even begin an ancestor wall or scrapbook. If you have photographs of deceased ancestors, display them. They should be displayed on your ancestor's altar.

Leave contributions that your forefathers and mothers may have cherished - food, beverages, jewels, stones, cigars, or anything else! For example, if you know that your great-grandpa smoked tobacco, consider leaving a bowl of tobacco as an offering. If you know your grandmother accumulated packets of sweet n' low, leave some out for her to stuff in her "purse." Invoking the assistance of ancestors will always result in a good end – but keep in mind that they, too, appreciate being appreciated for their favors!

Chapter 12

Five Prayers For Ancestors That Few People Consider At Samhain

So.

Heads up.

What we're discussing is neither simple nor enjoyable. There are times when you need to pause and contemplate. Slow down and allow yourself to feel true. Because if we are unable to experience things properly, we will be unable to discern what we genuinely need to do. We keep pushing forward, ever forward, accomplishing tasks to accomplish them. Allow yourself to lament on this, Samhain. That is its purpose.

Paying Tribute to Those Who Died Unjustly

It's all too simple to assume that unfair acts occurred in antiquity. We might express regret for those who perished in inquisitorial witch hunts or those who perished fighting in the Civil War. However, we can reflect on the people who perished in ancient wars and genocides and not be too concerned about the reality that horrible things continue to happen to people who do not deserve it regularly.

However, it does and has done so this year. According to the Southern Poverty Law Center, hate crimes are upswing. Other natural disasters have killed people in the United States, including wildfires and storms in the west and east. As a result, there are hate crimes, such as in Las Vegas. In addition, Syria's civil war continues.

Why bother remembering all of this negative information? Isn't it preferable to simply put everything behind you and move on?

It may benefit our mental health if we are lucky enough to do so. Nevertheless, should we?

If we are ever to overcome the problems that confront us, we must confront them squarely. We must learn how to be truthful. This is true in our daily lives just as it is true in the big arena of public policy: this Samhain, practice openness and acceptance of your feelings about these experiences. At the very least, those who passed deserve that much.

A Prayer for Those Who Sit With The Unjustly Murdered:

I address those who perished in blazing wars, those who desired simply the simplest things: the joy of the day and the serenity of the night.

Blessed is your memory, I say to those who have perished due to hatred. Others who have been harmed by belief, through distorted dread, have been released on those perceived as different.

Blessed is your memory, I say to those who died by the Mother's influence. Winds and storms fuelled fires, and the Earth's sweeping strength are all out of balance.

Blessed is your memory, I say to those who have perished due to hunger, preventable disease, or unwarranted harm. I address those who died impoverished and battling for survival.

Your memory is blessed.

I recall you. I am aware of you. I am not going to forget you. I will allow this truth to pass over and through me. I will remain available to fulfill the work I have been called.

Your memory is blessed.

Paying Tribute to Our African Ancestors

It makes no difference whether we practice Voudoo, Neo-Pagan Druidry, or Shinto; the reality is that humanity began in the African savannahs approximately 200,000 years ago (at the very least) and that we lived blissfully on the continent of Africa for approximately 120,000 years. We began to depart some 80,000 years ago. To put it another way, we were confined to Africa for more than half of Homo Sapiens' existence.

Archaeological evidence, such as their bones, artifacts, and cave paintings, provides insight into the beliefs of persons who lived in the past. For example, humans swimming and hunting giraffes are depicted in cave art in Libya and Algeria's Saharan Desert. Previously, the desert was a savannah, and humans lived on the entire continent. Perhaps by remembering our forefathers and mothers from so long ago, we might take a moment to appreciate our links to one another.

A Prayer for Our Forefathers and Mothers:

Most Eternal, I return your call through the great swaths of time!

From the dawn of recorded history,

Before the Romans' wars and conquests: City, Republic, and Empire

Cultures rich and extensive rose before cultivating the lush regions between the Euphrates and the Tigris.

Before the untamed steppe horses were tamed, you were there before the land bridge to the Americas was crossed.

We will never forget you, most ancient ones, on this day.

You and we are one, our DNA identical to yours.

Your intellect is brilliant and brilliant, your words are intelligent, and your hands function identically to ours.

We are grateful for your gifts and your survival.

We are you, returning to expand on your work as the sands of time shift.

Please accept our offering, most ancient ones, homo sapiens!

Our Miscarriages and Abortions Are To Be Honored

This, I believe, is the most difficult one to discuss. Additionally, many people may take issue with my grouping miscarriages and abortions together, but that is how I see it. Full disclosure: I've dealt with both, so I'm familiar with them. Each Samhain, I make three offerings in memory of the three times I've experienced that loss. Yes, there is a loss, even when the abortion is legal. It is a decision. This is not an easy decision. I prioritized the needs of those alive over the needs of those who might live, and I would do it again. I still cry about it and allow myself the space necessary for Samhain's mourning. It is a commendable endeavor for the many of us who have experienced that agony.

Numerous traditions say that infants who die before being baptized or ritually initiated into society are unquietly dead. I made a firm decision that mine would not be an uneasy one. They would be well-cared for and respected, which has been beneficial for me. I would argue that it was beneficial to them as well.

A prayer for those unable to enter this world entirely: I sing a pleasant tune for you, darling.

I sing a wonderful melody for you, who remained in the beyond's possibilities.

I was unable to bestow upon you the gifts of the body.

I was unable to share my days and my existence with you.

I was unable to provide you with flesh and blood that was mine.

I couldn't see or feel your gorgeous face or hand grab mine.

I wish I could have loved you, but that was not to be.

Hopefully, you'll make your way to the heavens or join the cheerful winds in their pranks.

May you be blessed by love, whether in the spirit realm or the realm of the living.

May your soul be sweet and happy, and may you find joy, serenity, and love wherever you go.

May you receive this offering on Samhain with the knowledge that you are remembered and cherished.

Honoring Extinct Species

We are human, and our concentration is primarily on human matters. That is how things are. However, there is a vast world of other species out there, and some are also in serious trouble. Certainly, squirrels and rubbish pandas may not require our assistance, but Polar Bears most likely do. Take time to reflect on those species that have ceased to exist on this planet. According to the spirit work I and others have done, the echoes of their spirits can be heard in the hereafter. I know individuals who work with extinct animal spirits. Therefore, reaching out to those spirits and providing them with offerings and care on your shrine at Samhain is worthwhile.

A prayer for Extinct Species:

Blessed are those with wings and hooves, green and red ancestors.

I address those who once lived on this planet but no longer did.

I summon the colossal ancient dinosaurs that roamed odd prehistoric jungles.

I address the dodo that lived and died and now remains only in photographs.

I appeal to the weird and the mundane. Each species is distinct and no longer fills a niche.

May the Mother recall you and keep you in her thoughts.

May the Earth sprout new species that are blessed in their unique ways.

May we remember and maintain the balance so that those who live may continue to live.

Honoring the Heroic Dead

I left this one till last since it is the most uplifting. I bring up these categories of the Dead to illustrate how tough they are to consider. Individuals and groups alike owe it on themselves to contemplate these losses. They are real, and if we do not make an effort to bring them into the light, they will remain hidden in our shadow selves.

The Heroic Dead are those who took action to alleviate that pain. They are the individuals who have impacted the lives of others. They are the ones who have contributed to making the world a little bit safer and a little bit more just. The heroic dead are those who lived their values deeply and courageously. There are a plethora of them. I pay tribute to Harriet Tubman, Ida B. Wells, Louisa May Alcott, Octavia Butler, and Carrie Fisher. Discover those who were courageous enough to act and read their experiences. I recommend visiting your local library and checking out a biography or autobiography for this one. Learn from your forefathers and mothers. Their wisdom can assist you in discovering your own.

A Prayer for the Heroic Dead:

I'm going to assist you in writing your own for this one.

To begin, make a list of all the virtues you believe in. It would be Courage, Integrity, Wisdom, Wit, Kindness, and Compassion.

Then consider some historical figures you respect that exemplify that. If you're at a loss for someone, conduct a Google search for quotations regarding your virtue. Scroll through the quotes until you discover one that strikes a chord with you, and then look up who said it. That is your individual. I've already mentioned my heroes, and I'm not going to do so again.

Then express how amazing they were and how you aspire to be just like them when you grow up—only more opulent. I'll provide an example, but you can implement it however you choose.

Then put everything together. Mine would look as follows:

Courage, Integrity, Wisdom, Intelligence, Dexterity, Kindness, and Compassion.

These are the virtues that I espouse.

This is my identity.

Ida B. Wells, Harriet Tubman, Louisa May Alcott, Octavia Butler, and Carrie Fisher.

These are the forefathers and mothers I admire.

This was their nature.

Their wisdom and example have blessed me. Their deeds move me. I shall do as they did; I will contribute to humanity's long history through my gifts and abilities. To commemorate their memory, I shall be a hero in my way, in my day.

So be it.

Chapter 13

Ways To Conduct Free
Family Tree Research

"How did you get here?" For the majority of individuals, this is a straightforward question. However, when conducting family history research, answering becomes a lengthy and occasionally arduous experience.

You might wind up looking through information bases and turning back the clock to fill in the holes whenever you've addressed second cousins and incredible grandparents. You might wind up looking through information bases and turning back the clock to fill in the holes whenever you've addressed second cousins and incredible grandparents. However, before spending money on genealogy research, look at the following sites.

Each provides an abundance of knowledge for free. You may discover everything necessary to complete your family tree, from birth certificates and wills to census data and images.

1. Public libraries

This may surprise you, but tracing your family history may be as simple as visiting your local library.

Libraries across the country provide free access to popular genealogy websites to cardholders.

In Florida, for example, the Boca Raton Public Library subscribes to Ancestry Library Edition, which Ancestry.com powers. Residents with a library account may access the service in person at the library.

Investigate genealogy research alternatives on your local library's website or contact the library directly.

2. Genealogy Center at the Allen County Public Library

Due to the breadth of its databases, the Allen County Public Library Genealogy Center in Fort Wayne, Indiana, warrants its mention.

They cover Allen County, the entire state of Indiana, and neighboring states. Additionally, they feature materials for military veterans, Native Americans, and African Americans.

The nicest part is that a library card is not required. Free databases from the genealogical center can be accessed online.

3. National Archives

Civilian records are housed at the National Archives and Records Administration.

Those frequently utilized for genealogy research include the following:

- Census records

- Military service records

- Records relating to immigration

- Naturalization records

- Records of federal government transfers of public lands to private ownership

4. Liberty Statue-Ellis Island Foundation

The Statue of Liberty-Ellis Island Foundation's resources include records on millions of people who entered the United States via the Port of New York between 1820 and 1957.

These data are available for research at the American Family Immigration History Center, housed within the Ellis Island National Museum of Immigration and on the foundation's website.

5. The USGenWeb Project

The USGenWeb Project identifies itself as "a collection of genealogists united by a common goal of developing free online resources for genealogical research."

The national website of the project provides links to its state websites, which in turn provide links to county webpages. These websites make available a variety of resources, including the following:

- Listings of local sources for records

- County and state histories

- Online genealogy books

- Research tips

- Maps

- Links to other resources

6. AccessGenealogy

AccessGenealogy has the most comprehensive collection of free genealogical resources in the United States, including hundreds of thousands of free websites.

However, it specializes in Native American history and genealogy.

7. AfriGeneas

AfriGeneas is a genealogy website devoted to African Americans. The site contains photographs, a slave data collection, a surname database, and marriage and death records databases.

8. FamilySearch

Founded roughly 100 years ago in Salt Lake City, Utah, the Church of Jesus Christ of Latter-day Saints-affiliated FamilySearch has grown into a website with 238 users worldwide.

You may search the non-billions profit of records and build your family tree by registering a free account at FamilySearch.org.

9. Locate A Grave

If you're beginning your genealogy search, Find A Grave contains information about and photographs of gravesites donated by community members – individuals who have created a free Find A Grave account.

You can utilize the site to build your monument or to search through the site's 210 million existing tributes.

10. Chronicling America

The United States Library of Congress and the National Endowment for the Humanities jointly fund Chronicling America. This website allows access to digitized newspaper pages dating from 1777 to 1963 to reveal an intriguing tidbit about a relative.

Use the Advanced Search tab to look up a family member's name and filter the results by state and date period.

With this thorough guide, you'll learn everything you need to know to achieve your retirement goals.

The Single Most Important Retirement Guide You'll Ever Need provides you with the information necessary to retire on your terms. While you can hire a financial consultant, this online course gives you complete control over creating a customized retirement plan centered on the activities that bring you joy.

You're going to receive expert, tailored counsel. You'll get access to cutting-edge technology. And after you've completed it, you'll be able to approach retirement with confidence and peace of mind.

Simple Methods for Beginning
Your Family History Discovery

Have you ever wondered whether your ancestors influenced who you are today? Our friends at Findmypast offer some excellent recommendations to assist you in determining this.

Family history encompasses far more than names and dates. It's about discovering your roots and learning about your forefathers and mothers. As with the celebrities on 'Who Do You Think You Are?' there will be surprises, disclosures, and twists and turns. You can stumble across secrets and scandals. But, most importantly, it's about embarking on an enthralling, occasionally emotional, but always gratifying path of self-discovery that is unique to you.

You are the investigator when it comes to family history. This tutorial illuminates some of the issues you can anticipate as you explore your past. With real-life experiences from actual people, straightforward guidance on getting started, and information on the types of things you can accomplish, the only question you'll have is why you didn't start sooner.

Why is family history important?

There are a huge number of valid justifications to dive into our pasts. To begin, it's now simpler than ever before to get started. Genealogy used to entail cross-country visits to archive offices in the hope of finding what you were looking for. Now, everything is accessible with a single mouse click or app tap.

Family history is one of those hobbies that can become (somewhat) addicted. However, when 'just 15 more minutes' evolves into the wee hours of the morning, keep in mind that you may have far worse habits.

As with solving a crossword puzzle, completing a Sudoku puzzle, or guessing whodunnit, piecing together the puzzle of your past is replete with satisfying 'Eureka' moments. After all, who doesn't enjoy pretending to be a detective?!

Above all, investigating your family tree is the only way to gain a true understanding of your ancestors. Possessing that knowledge has the potential to alter your current and future significantly. Along the process, you'll be able to read your ancestor's school records, locate them in historical newspapers, learn about their occupation, and much more. Whatever you do, do not allow their stories to fade into obscurity.

How to begin your family tree:

Now that you understand why family history is critical, the next step is determining where to begin. But, again, these straightforward suggestions serve as excellent jumping-off points.

1. Put your current knowledge into a list.

Create a simple family tree in which you are the root. Begin with your close family and work your way up. Include as many dates and locations as possible for births, marriages, and deaths. This will draw attention to any gaps in your knowledge. For example, are you familiar with the women's maiden names? What about the jobs of men? All of this will assist you in identifying the correct individuals when you begin your search for family records.

2. Inquire of your relatives

Your family's narrative begins at home. Present your initial try at a family tree to your closest relatives to see if they can help you fill in any gaps. Inquire about their memories of deceased family members. Are there any family rumors that warrant further investigation? Is there any criminality or aristocratic ties? Who served in the military? Make a list. These lines of inquiry will direct you to the next step.

3. Begin your rummaging

Bring down that dusty box from the attic and search for old documents or photographs. National identification cards, driver's licenses, passports, and letters may contain sensitive information.

Take note of ages, addresses, and occupations, and update your family tree with any new information you discover.

4. Conduct research online.

Now that you've laid the groundwork, it's time to delve a little deeper. On websites such as findmypast.co.uk, you may access millions of birth, marriage, death, and census information.

They'll uncover the most vital elements of your family's history and arm you with the necessary information to go further back.

5. Preserve your findings

Online family tree builders let you include every significant event in your ancestors' lives and supporting documents and photographs. By creating your family tree online, you ensure that it will be securely saved for the foreseeable future. So what's the best part? Begin and expand your family tree online for free at Findmypast.

6. Old news is often the best news

Local newspapers covered everything from drunken brawls to new births and company openings. Your forebears are almost certain to be referenced in Findmypast's massive newspaper archive. The real question is why they made headlines.

7. Pay tribute to family heroes

Most of us know whether our forefathers or mothers served, but few are aware of much more.

Military records can shed light on every aspect of your relative's service, allowing you to understand their experiences and sacrifices truly.

8. Follow in your forefathers' and mothers' footsteps

Complete addresses can be found in censuses and other historical documents. Utilize these to plan a visit to your relatives' former residences. Seeing these historic homes is certain to raise the hairs on your neck.

Consider what you might learn...

Every day, millions of people are tracing their family lineages. These enthralling tales will encourage you to begin your own.

Chapter 14

What Is Intergenerational Trauma, And How Do You Heal?

Numerous beneficial traits can be passed down via families – your sense of humor, customs, and cherished experiences, to name a few. However, mental injury can be passed down across generations. A process is known as generational trauma.

Alternatively referred to as intergenerational trauma, generational trauma is an emotional wound that passes from generation to generation. Finally, hereditary trauma affects individuals, families, and communities long-term.

According to Alfie Breland-Noble, Ph.D., MHSc, psychologist, author, and founder of the AAKOMA Project, "it's a set of experiences and behaviors tied to events that occurred many years ago; to someone in your family."

However, the cycle can be broken: It is possible that recovering from any form of trauma is a lengthy process.

To assist, the following is an overview of intergenerational trauma, including what it is, how it manifests, who is affected, and how to begin healing.

Generational Trauma: What Is It?

Vivian M. Rakoff, MD, a Canadian psychiatrist, was among the first to investigate the definition of generational trauma in 1966, after observing a high rate of psychiatric distress among offspring of Holocaust survivors, according to the American Psychological Association (APA).

According to Duke University, the word has since developed to broadly apply trauma passed from generation to generation via biological, social, and psychological variables.

Any traumatic incident that results in significant distress can be transmitted. According to the APA, the following is a non-exhaustive list of experiences that might result in generational trauma:

- Systemic and cultural oppression

- War

- Genocide

- Poverty

- Slavery

- Assault or abuse

For example, a parent may be unable to provide emotional support to a child who has been sexually attacked if the parent has not processed their own abuse experience. Alternatively, a grandparent who refuses to confront their traumatic experience fighting in a war may educate their grandkids to disregard and minimize their emotional difficulties.

Vicarious suffering is another critical component of intergenerational trauma. "Trauma is not just about the terrible incident," Breland-Noble explains. "It is also about our response to the event." "Observing something while having the sensation of being directly involved in it is what I mean by first-person experience."

The following are examples of intergenerational trauma, as defined by the Association for Child and Adolescent Mental Health (ACAMH):

- Unresolved feelings and thoughts about the traumatic experience

- Impaired parent-child connections

- Complicated personality features or personality disorders

- Negative repeated patterns of behavior

Intergenerational trauma also has bodily consequences. For instance, according to a February 2021 study published in the International Journal of Environmental Research and Public Health, historical trauma, stress, and racism are all associated with an increased incidence of cardiometabolic disease among Indigenous communities.

Concerns about parenthood or the child's health during pregnancy, according to the study, can have long-term physical impacts on both the mother and the child, such as low birth weight, premature delivery, and gestational diabetes.

Intergenerational trauma research is still in its infancy, and this is only the tip of the iceberg in terms of findings. Nonetheless, Ajita Robinson, Ph.D., grief and trauma therapist and author of The Gift of Grief, feels the term is gaining popularity.

"The public has gained awareness of the phrase generational trauma and can discern its manifestations in their own lived experiences," Robinson explains. "[Millennials] grew up in a culture that normalized mental health — they can articulate that certain behaviors and familial customs are founded in trauma."

Tip

Contrary to popular assumption, employing toxic positivity to minimize one's experiences and feelings can impede one's ability to process trauma, according to a study published in Educational Development in Times of Crises in 2021.

Intergenerational Trauma Affects Whom?

Trauma is a prevalent occurrence. Take a look at the figures provided by the National Council for Behavioral Health:

- Approximately 70% of adults in the United States have encountered at least one traumatic event.

- Around 90% of children who are sexually abused develop post-traumatic stress disorder.

- Over 90% of those who suffer from behavioral health disorders have been exposed to trauma.

And, like other forms of trauma, intergenerational trauma can affect anyone. However, certain groups are disproportionately impacted.

For example, historically oppressed groups such as LGBTQIA+ people, Black people, Indigenous people, and people of color are particularly vulnerable as a result of historical trauma, a type of intergenerational trauma experienced by a particular cultural, racial, or ethnic group, according to the Administration for Children and Families (ACF).

The consequences of significant historical events such as slavery, forced migration, the Holocaust, and the harsh colonialism of Indigenous peoples may still be felt.

According to the ACF, due to historical and contemporary systematic oppression and brutality, Black people and other people of color frequently fear the world around them.

This fear, for example, maybe evident in both the dread and obligation that Black parents have faced while discussing future police confrontations with their children.

Communities that have experienced historical trauma are also vulnerable to race-based traumatic stress, which Mental Health America defines as emotional damage produced by interactions with racism.

For instance, an April 2014 study published in the journal Cultural Diversity and Ethnic Minority Psychology discovered a relationship between racial discrimination at school and depressive symptoms in Black teenagers.

Race-related traumatic stress manifests itself in the workplace as well. Researchers examined how racism and sexism affect Black women at work in an older but still relevant June 2011 study published in the Journal of Black Studies (the study uses "women"). The research discovered that typical work-related stressors include the following:

- Code-switching to overcome employment restrictions

- Coping with racial harassment and racism

- Being alone and ostracized

- Defending one's race

- Lack of mentorship

Because of institutional racism, Black people are more likely to experience stressful work environments than their white counterparts. And this excessive quantity of stress may contribute to worse mental and cardiovascular health.

According to a September 2016 study published in Psychological Trauma: Theory, Research, Practice, and Policy, race-based traumatic stress is also associated with increased anxiety, hypervigilance, guilt, shame, avoidance, and numbing.

Tip

It's critical to realize that intergenerational trauma can be exacerbated for those with several marginalized identities. "As a Black or Latinx queer person, you must contend with not only racism but also homophobia and transphobia," Breland-Noble explains.

How Do We Begin the Healing Process Following Intergenerational Trauma?

Breaking the cycle of inherited harm can aid in the healing process following intergenerational trauma. As a starting point, here are some ideas:

1. Identify Your Trauma

You can take a significant first step toward healing by vocalizing your trauma.

"We must identify the effects of intergenerational trauma on us," Breland-Noble argues. "There are times when you must name it to yourself because the people you care about are not prepared to hear it."

Recognizing that you have been a victim of trauma might then assist you in processing the emotions associated with it.

2. Claim Your Trauma

While you are not required to embrace or make peace with your trauma, denying that it occurred can make it even more difficult to absorb.

"You do not have to accept your trauma, but you must acknowledge its existence and then take action," Breland-Noble explains.

3. Engage in Self-Care

Taking action to address your trauma might begin with addressing your emotional wellbeing through self-care activities that resonate with you. According to Breland-Noble, the following strategies should be used:

- Guided meditation

- Exercise

- Nutrient-dense foods

- Consumption of media that inspires you

4. Permit Relationships to Adapt

When your trauma is related to someone you care about, ending the relationship or establishing the boundaries necessary to feel safe is not always simple.

"When a relationship is ready to alter, end, or evolve in a new way, we must allow it to happen," Breland-Noble says. "With intergenerational trauma, we sometimes accept people's actions out of love, but you must gradually establish limits. By doing so, you increase your own space."

5. Allow for Grief

Ending the cycle of intergenerational trauma may result in disenfranchised sorrow, in which you may feel a sense of loss even if no one died.

"Trauma work must be conducted concurrently with grief work," Robinson explains. "Inevitably, as we peel back the layers of trauma, we are confronted with the necessity of 'grieving the gap' between what we received and what we required."

6. Seek Assistance

You are not required to confront your trauma alone, so receiving help can be life-changing. This can take consulting a mental health professional or becoming a supportive community member.

Therapy has historically been stigmatized in BIPOC groups, so it's critical to find a culturally competent therapist, Breland-Noble explains. "That way, you're not always explaining your origin and culture," she explains.

Therapy can help you process your feelings, but it can also assist you in coping with the physical consequences of trauma." " As a trauma therapist, I help my clients learn how to 'be in their bodies' because trauma typically involves numbness, disembodiment, and escape. Additionally, she urges individuals to develop the skills necessary to help them regulate their emotions and navigate distress.

And, if treatment is not a possibility, Robinson proposes locating or creating a group of like-minded individuals. "For some, this may take the form of spiritual or religious settings; for others, it may take the form of online groups centered on wellbeing," she explains.

CONCLUSION

How different cultures honor their ancestors is as varied as the civilizations themselves. For example, to honor their ancestors in Mexico, they would pour a small amount of alcohol on the ground. The people from the Far East culture place the bones of ancestors beneath their homes. Because other cultures believe that their ancestors are still alive, they do not bury them.

Every cell in our body is conscious in many of my channeling sessions and other sources.

To understand the nature of the matter is to realize that it has other, hidden truths. As an illustration, consider that we can see and feel a person's physical body. In addition to this, we know that a person has feelings that we can only detect when they express them verbally. In addition, invisible beings such as ghosts and psyches can be observed through their behaviors rather than the naked eye. And so forth. As a result, we only get to view a sliver of the big picture at any given time. And that our bodies are only a little part of a much greater system. Our forefathers are still alive and intertwined with us but out of sight.

Ancestors can be a powerful source of inspiration.

First, you have to recreate the rhythm and harmony of your town when you start making contact with the spirits of your ancestors. In what way is this relevant? It implies a second culture that includes your family and ancestors that you are unaware of.

When you touch with your ancestors, you gain access to their wisdom and information. Mysterious events may not be involved. As a result, you may be startled by the opportunities presented. You may meet new people who will be there for you in good times and bad.

You will be shielded from view. You are in touch with your physical sensations when connecting with your ancestors. You might not want to eat something unhealthy if you don't think it's good for you. You may avoid certain routes, certain types of people with ulterior motivations, and other potentially unsafe spots.

Your ancestors lived in the realm of unseen energies, and every place, object, or person gives off certain types of vibrational energies where they can hide these energetic scents. Still, they can't hide it on higher energetic levels, whenever even a person's intention gives off a certain frequency. When you've fully connected with your ancestors, so, even if you don't see your ancestors, they'll guide you down the right path; they can make you late to keep you from getting into an accident; they can cause a minor accident to keep you from attending a particular date, or they can make your friend lost so that they can't invite you to a party that could harm you.

You only have to look at how parents shield their infants and toddlers from fire, pits, and dirt. You will be guided and protected in the same way your ancestors have done for generations. Spiritual and psychic attacks aren't the only types of attacks that could occur.

Some disorders may be traced back to our genes, which is fascinating to notice. Unresolved conflicts inside or between your family tree or with other ancestors are indicated by this, as you are well aware. This indicates a potential energy obstruction in your family tree that needs to be addressed.

When a member of one family marries another family with an unresolved ancestral dispute, it can lead to miscarriages, birth deformities, and other health problems, all because the two families' issues were never resolved in the past.

However, if a ceremony is held, the issue is resolved. It's possible that even these diseases can be triggered by family tension. It's possible that one brother robbed the other or that a brother's wife had an affair with a sibling. As a result of unresolved disagreements, physical ailments can develop. Connecting with your ancestors allows you to see these things, and you can easily resolve them once you are aware of them.

Your ancestors are eagerly awaiting your call.

Many ways to connect with your ancestors are at your disposal. In most circumstances, your ancestors will reach out to you if you need them. Dreams are the primary mode of transportation. The memories of my departed grandfather haunted me as a child. He took me to many other places and taught me a lot. A few days after realizing it was all a dream, he passed away.

- If you don't, you'll never be able to embrace them in your heart and accept that they exist.

- You might begin by reconnecting with your family's history and culture. Be curious about your ancestry once in a while and learn a little about the culture and traditions that shaped who you are.

- Place a piece of classic art in your living space. Inviting your ancestors to share your place through the arts. Everything from paintings to sculptures to furniture can be considered art. What it's like to have a Star Wars enthusiast come over to your house and discover that you have a lightsaber on your wall. Those who know you best will take a personal interest in your progress.

- Traditional festivals are worth checking out. The atmosphere at heritage festivals is always pleasant. A wise spirit may notice your hobbies and shine a light on you.

- Find the items of your ancestors to communicate with them. As long as it's an image, it's acceptable.

- You can identify a date that links you to your ancestors if you commemorate. Their birthdate, a holiday, or a Sunday if they used to go to church are all possibilities. The deceased's spirit can guide you in any way, from lighting a candle to visiting their graves to planting a plant in their honor.

In conclusion, we feel less isolated and abandoned as soon as we acknowledge our ancestors' presence in our lives. Many people are terrified of the practice of connecting with our ancestors because the church has stigmatized this practice of connecting with our forefathers.

If our late forefathers were the devil, they would have damaged us while still alive, but they weren't. Every day, Roman Catholics offer prayers to their patron saints. No, these saints aren't just ghosts. Why is it different for you if you want to connect with your ancestors?

In addition, some people have had a painful experience with their family, such as their father being abusive or their Mother being abusive, which can impact their mental health. Healing oneself and forgiving oneself are the most important aspects of this situation. What happened to you can be healed if you let go of it and see it from a distance to understand its fundamental reason.

Dear Reader,

As independent authors it's often difficult to gather reviews compared with much bigger publishers.

Therefore, please leave a review on the platform where you bought this book.

Many thanks,

Author Team

Want Free New Book Launches?

Email "Ancestral Veneration" at:

mindsetmastership@gmail.com